P9-DDU-517

CHRISTIAN FAITH
AND PUBLIC CHOICES

North Carolina Wesleyan College Library

Scurry - Drum
Collection
Given by:
Dr. Frank Scurry and
Carolina Evangelical
Divinity School

CHRISTIAN FAITH AND PUBLIC CHOICES

The Social Ethics of Barth, Brunner, and Bonhoeffer

ROBIN W. LOVIN

FORTRESS PRESS   PHILADELPHIA

NC WESLEYAN COLLEGE
ELIZABETH BRASWELL PEARSALL LIBRARY

Biblical quotations from *The New English Bible,* © The Delegates of the
Oxford University Press and The Syndics of the Cambridge University
Press, 1961, 1970, are used by permission.

Biblical quotations from the Revised Standard Version of the Bible,
copyright 1946, 1952, © 1971, 1973 by the Division of Christian Education of the National Council of the Churches of Christ in the U.S.A. are
used by permission.

COPYRIGHT © 1984 BY FORTRESS PRESS

All rights reserved. No part of this publication may be reproduced,
stored in a retrieval system, or transmitted in any form or by any means,
electronic, mechanical, photocopying, recording, or otherwise, without
the prior permission of the copyright owner.

Library of Congress Cataloging in Publication Data

Lovin, Robin W.
  Christian faith and public choices.

  Includes index.
  1. Christian ethics—History—20th century. 2. Social
ethics—History—20th century. 3. Barth, Karl, 1886–1968.
4. Brunner, Emil, 1889–1966. 5. Bonhoeffer, Dietrich,
1906–1945. I. Title.
BJ1231.L68 1984   241'.0404'0922   83–48922
ISBN 0–8006–1777–0

K474K83   PRINTED IN THE UNITED STATES OF AMERICA   1–1777

CONTENTS

PREFACE

This is a book about three figures whose reputations as theologians have obscured their importance for ethics. Barth, Brunner, and Bonhoeffer all took polemical pleasure in denouncing ethics and ethicists. Ethicists have usually returned the compliment.

The result is that apart from those occasions when Anglo-American writers trot them out as exemplars of "situation ethics," the three theologians are rarely studied for their ethics. Christology and ecclesiology dominate the secondary literature, with some attention to their preaching and their methods of biblical interpretation. Yet Barth, Brunner, and Bonhoeffer did all their theology against a backdrop of social crisis and personal commitments that made them very much aware of the moral dimension that pervades their work. In this study, I have tried to highlight that dimension and to show how it shapes the intellectual relationships between the three.

Many colleagues have helped with this book. Jonathan Gosser insisted fifteen years ago that I had to read Bonhoeffer. He was right. David Tracy, Martin Marty, and Jerald Brauer have all read pieces of this project and encouraged me in it. I have learned more from James Gustafson than I can properly footnote, but readers who know his recent work on Barth will recognize its influence in these pages.

Colleagues in ministry have helped, too. Gene Winkler gave me an opportunity to teach some of this material in his congregation. Pastor Patrick McNally and the people of my "base community" at Epworth United Methodist Church in Chicago have heard these themes in sermons and study groups, and they have supported the work in ways they would not guess.

Most of all, I am grateful to students at the Divinity School of the University of Chicago. They signed up for a course obscurely titled

"Theological Ethics between the Wars." They said they liked it, and they said they learned something from it. One thing they said they learned was a set of questions that helped them to read contemporary Christian ethics differently. I will be satisfied if readers of this book can say the same.

Chicago, Illinois   ROBIN W. LOVIN
June 26, 1983

1
CHRISTIAN FAITH
AND PUBLIC CHOICES

The history of ethics seldom provides direct moral answers, but it may help us understand our fundamental moral questions. If we must decide how to regulate genetic experimentation, protect the environment for future generations, or end the economic dependency of the less-developed nations, we will need information and analyses that grow old in weeks or years, not decades or centuries. But if we reflect also on what it means to make public moral decisions on these issues, we will need insights of a different sort. We will need to understand how our fundamental beliefs about reality shape all of the more specific choices we make, and we will need to think about how we relate to other persons who will also have to join us in the decisions, whether or not they share our beliefs.

Karl Barth, Emil Brunner, and Dietrich Bonhoeffer are important for Christian ethics today because they help us with this second problem. Often they have no advice on specific questions we ask, and at other times we will find the advice they give hopelessly outdated. What they do have to offer is an understanding of the fundamental choices we must make before we can relate Christian faith to any particular decision.

The power of Barth, Brunner, and Bonhoeffer to shape theology in the ninth and tenth decades of this century as they shaped it in the third and fourth lies in their confrontation with the basic questions that must be answered before our responses to the smaller questions that dog our daily steps will make any sense. Before Christians can decide that an abortion law is "antifamily" or that a school board's decisions violate parents' rights, they have to have some notion of what the family is supposed to be in God's creation and how that family relates to other institutions—schools and states, shops and churches—that are also part of the world we are given. Before we can say that limiting nuclear weapons or abolishing capital punishment or freeing political prisoners is doing the will of God, we have to have some confidence that we can know the will of God, and we have to have some ideas about how we know it. Barth, Brunner, and Bonhoeffer remain important for theology today because they addressed specific problems without losing sight of the larger questions. We will find in the course of this study that their answers to these fundamental questions were by no means the same. Indeed, it is precisely the differences between them that will help us to decide what those questions are. Barth wrote vigorously against Brunner's approach to ethics, and in later years he confessed his puzzlement at much of what Bonhoeffer had written. Bonhoeffer and Brunner each criticized Barth, and though I will argue that their two positions are very much alike, they would no doubt have had complaints to lodge against each other. This is not a book about a single "school" of Christian thought but an examination of a white-hot argument which I will try to present in ways that shed light on our own situation.

Ethics and Obedience

The problem for Barth, Brunner, and Bonhoeffer was not this or that ethical problem but whether Christianity can provide any basis for moral action in society. This problem had particular force for historical reasons, which we will examine later in this chapter, but it is a recurrent problem in Christian thought. Certain features of moral choice and action as modern thinkers understand them simply do not readily cohere with the requirements of faith and obedience to God. Rousseau suggested that the moral problem is how one can be joined to society and "still obey himself alone, and remain as free as before."[1] John Courtney Murray insisted that for Christians the problem of social ethics is to maintain "the sovereignty of God over nations as well as over individual men."[2] Between that assertion of human autonomy and that insistence on divine sovereignty, the problem falls. Religious ethics in the modern world that Rousseau and his Enlightenment followers made must address the problem of individuality and society in a way that does not compromise the freedom and initiative of God.

Ethics in the modern world is fundamentally a discipline of giving public reasons for action. The way we respect the autonomy of persons in our social decisions is by inviting their consent on essential choices, rather than forcing them to conform or deluding them with propaganda. To make a moral argument is to state one's case in terms that require others either to concur in the choice or to offer better reasons for rejecting it. Moral argument is thus quite different from explaining my choices in terms of my own preferences or merely announcing what I intend to do. Statements of preferences and declarations of intent allow you to predict my behavior and may help you to understand it, but they do not require a response from you in the same way that a moral argument does.

If giving moral reasons helps to resolve Rousseau's problem of individual autonomy and social cooperation, it is not immediately clear that theological reasons are or can be moral. A theological reason may explain the believer's choice, but it demands a corresponding choice only from those who share the theology. If I declare my opposition to capital punishment because I believe in a forgiving God who never puts any person beyond the reach of repentance and renewal of life, someone may quite well respond, "I know perfectly well what you mean; and if I believed the world were that way, I would certainly agree with you; but I find the world the sort of place where people are apt to try to get away with anything; and our only effective defense is a system of swift and severe punishments that will discourage others from trying it, too."

Theological affirmations make poor premises for public moral arguments precisely because they are held by a limited group of the faithful, while a moral argument aims to establish a general obligation. The theologians may wish to offer an explanation so winsome and inspiring that others will want to share it. They may even believe, as Barth did, that all persons eventually *will* share it. For the moment, however, they must acknowledge that their vision is only one among many that compete for attention.

> Now it is true that, according to Philippians 2:11, the vocative "Father" will finally, as the goal of the rule and work of Jesus Christ, be the word of all men and indeed of all creation ringing out in the harmony of universal invocation. On this side of the eschaton, however, it is only one note among many other invocations and exclamations that are hardly in harmony with it, but call for notice just as loudly—or even more so. Here and now, in anticipation of the future universal praise of God, it is the affair of only a certain number of people, even a limited minority, to call God "Father."[3]

To address the Christian God as Father affirms that self-giving love is central in reality and expresses a trust that acts of compassion and reconciliation are, not heroic protests against an unforgiving universe, but appropriate responses to what has already been done for us.

3

Christians cannot surrender these distinctive claims. Yet the more clearly and directly they guide their actions by this "minority report," the greater the risk of finding their actions at odds with neighbors who make their choices only with reference to commonly held beliefs that can be checked against the facts.

Public Moral Choices

A moral argument intends to impose obligations on persons generally. It is a claim that here and now they all ought to do or to refrain from doing certain things, and it is a claim that they can understand the reasons for doing or for abstaining here and now, apart from other things they do or do not believe and apart from anything else they may come to believe in the future. That is the first of several points we may identify that make the discussion of moral questions a public issue that cannot be settled by appeal to the beliefs of a prophetic minority. The public moral claims may be quite limited, amounting to little more than a demand that others respect my rights, that is, refrain from actions that interfere with my efforts to understand, teach, and live a faith they do not share. Other public claims call for positive action or impose obligations on people in certain situations, as when we say that everyone should tell the truth or that people who receive favors should show gratitude to their benefactors. One philosopher has called these generally accepted rules for action prima facie duties.[4] We may argue about the specifics to which they apply (Must I tell the truth when Aunt Sally asks if I like her new hat?), but we do not doubt that these claims for action are addressed to all persons. In that respect, they are public in a way quite different from an argument that Christians ought to oppose capital punishment because Christ's promise of forgiveness and the possibility of repentance extend to all persons, even the worst offenders among them.

A second characteristic of modern moral arguments that poses difficulties for theology is that moral arguments involve generalizations about action. Like arguments in a court of law, public moral arguments identify characteristics of disputed choices that make them like accepted instances of gratitude or truth telling, for example. A moral argument establishes that this particular action is something we ought to do because it is like a larger class of actions that we agree ought to be performed. The status of general moral rules is a much-disputed question in ethical theory, and it is not hard to cite cases in which rigid adherence to a rule has produced results which are both unhappy and

4

difficult to defend. Nevertheless, it is difficult to see how public moral discussions can proceed at all without generalizations about either the sort of acts we ought to perform or the sort of results at which we ought to aim. Human beings have limited understandings. We cannot classify every possible action minutely to know it as a unique event, nor can we follow the consequences of our specific choices very far into the future. If we are to make our own decisions, it must be by generalization and analogy. We can "obey ourselves" only insofar as we are able to classify possible actions according to some rough table of duties. We must try to make our present hard choices as much as possible like the right choices we have made in the past. Of course, we could escape this difficult process of moral deliberation by choosing simply to follow in every specific instance the advice of some mentor or the commands of a superior authority, but modern moral philosophy would not count those as moral choices at all, and the record of Nuremberg and other war crimes trials is that humanity will not accept it as a substitute for personal moral accountability.

Christian ethics and especially Protestant ethics, however, link moral accountability with obedience to the command of God, and it is precisely the readiness for an encounter with the divine command that violates all ordinary expectations which Barth, Brunner, and Bonhoeffer want to preserve. Even Bonhoeffer, who of the three has perhaps the most respect for the philosophical heritage of the Enlightenment, questions the moral generalizations that are the basis for public scrutiny of moral choices. "The ethical, in this sense of the formal, the universally valid, and the rational contained no element of concretion, and it therefore inevitably ended in the total atomization of human society and of the life of the individual, in unlimited subjectivism and individualism."[5]

Probably the first unqualified generalization in Christian ethics was "We must obey God rather than men" (Acts 5:29). But if following that principle entails an immediate reliance on God's command that rejects the moral generalizations by which ordinary moral discourse moves, it is not clear how Christians can participate in public choices.

Moral discussions are public, then, in that they establish obligations that apply to persons generally, and they proceed by making generalizations about action. This suggests a third characteristic: public moral discussions invite general participation. A theocratic leadership that studies sacred texts and hands down a set of rules that apply to the populace generally has not thereby held a moral discussion, even if the rules it hands down are general rules. Because the logic of the generalizations by which moral disputes are settled can be understood by all rational persons, philosophers have usually considered that all those whom we hold fully accountable to moral standards (generally adults of sound reason) are likewise entitled to participate in formulating the standards. By contrast, we are often inclined to think that religious questions, even when they are publicly understood, can properly be settled only by those who participate in the community of faith. Christian scholars may think they understand very well what is at stake in a question of Islamic or Jewish law, but they will not usually regard themselves as qualified to resolve the question. Public moral issues allow no such barriers to participation. This does not preclude a special role in moral discussions for those of superior wisdom or wider experience, but it does suggest that their qualifications must, in principle, be confirmed by the other participants' agreement with their conclusions.

Moral discussions of conduct, then, have characteristics that make them public in a specially rigorous way. They commend or command actions on the basis of reasons understandable to persons generally; they evaluate actions by generalizations about acts or goals, and they make these generalizations in ways that permit general participation in the discussion. A discussion can be public in this way even when the conduct in question is not a matter of public policy. We often want to defend a course of personal action in these terms. When we explain why we limit our consumption of red meat or why we turned in a coworker who was cheating the company, we do not want merely to be understood. We want to be right. The response we want is not "Of course, that's what a Christian (or a Buddhist or a Methodist or a Mormon) would do," but "That's what anyone in that situation ought to do." That happens, however, only when we open our private choices to public discussion, when we are prepared to accept the scrutiny of those who may not share all of our starting points for thinking about human life and reality. We often submit ourselves to that discipline because we want our personal choices to make a moral point, but the public characteristics of moral discussions are crucial when the choice is a societal decision that must be made or endorsed by large numbers of people. In religious discussions of conduct, by contrast, the characteristics that make moral discussion public are often missing, and appropriately so. In modern pluralistic societies, it is hard to conceive of a religious community that asks nothing of its members beyond observance of the general ideas of virtue that prevail in the culture around them.

The problem that specially concerned European Protestants in the social confusion that followed World War I thus proves upon examination to be a general problem for Christian faith in the modern world. Faith begins with the will of God, while moral discourse begins with human freedom. Both must say how their starting points can be reconciled with the requirements of human life in society, but it is not clear that both can be reconciled in the same way. Both religious communities and society at large hold discussions of human choice and conduct, discussions which they call *ethics*. Once the religious community and the society are no longer simply identical, we are uncertain about how those two discussions are related.[6]

The End of the Liberal Era

The distinction between Christian faith and the moral choices of the wider society is not always equally apparent. Sometimes the two are so much alike that faith and civic loyalty seem like two sides of the same coin. At other times, the values of the wider society seem to collapse, and Christian thinkers struggle to discover what is distinctive in their faith that can be salvaged from the social disaster.

Barth and Brunner began their important work when Protestant Christianity in Europe was struggling with the social disorder that followed World War I, and their first theological task was to identify the Christian message and to disentangle it from a host of other ideas that had suddenly been discredited. The political system of the German Empire, European confidence in human progress, and a code of military honor had all enjoyed religious sanction in the very recent past. Now these concepts were discredited, and, unless Christian faith could be distinguished from them, that faith, too, might become a casualty of the postwar social crisis.

Making the necessary distinctions was not easy, for it meant a rejection of a whole way of thinking about Christianity which had dominated Protestantism, particularly in Germany, during the nineteenth century. This "liberal" theology tended to minimize the fixed, dogmatic content of Christianity and to focus instead on the experiences that inspire faith and deepen commitment to the Christian tradition. Both Christian dogmas and social values were viewed as imperfect, changing, historical realities, but nineteenth century theology also had confidence that both faith and culture were developing rapidly toward new forms that would eradicate any differences between them.

World War I brought an abrupt end to this European vision of social and religious progress. For the vanquished Central Powers political collapse and economic chaos came close on the heels of military defeat, and even the victorious Allies had suffered unprecedented death and destruction that shook intellectual confidence in the cultural foundations. Theology was implicated in these changes, not only in the sense that theologians are always marked in some way by the problems their societies face, but in the more specific sense that Protestant theology of the nineteenth century had bound itself quite willingly to European culture and European progress.

What marks Barth, Brunner, Bonhoeffer, and the other theologians of this period, then, is their sudden confrontation with the differences between Christian faith and cultural values. The first problem for Christian ethics after World War I was not to respond to this or that question of social policy, but to ask how—or whether—those public questions could be raised at all in a Christian context. Three major responses emerged, and it will help us to follow the development of Protestant thought after Barth to outline each of them briefly. The first, Christian socialism, continued the hopes of an earlier era for the historical reconciliation of Christianity and culture, though it envisioned that synthesis in quite different terms from those of liberal theology. The second, crisis theology, accented the irreducible distinction between the life of faith and society's moral choices. The third, which we will here call theological realism, recognized the difficulties in the idea that history would itself move society toward the realization of permanent values but sought an alternative foundation that would permit theology to speak meaningfully to social change and social choices.

Christian Socialism

We will deal most extensively in this chapter with the Christian socialism exemplified by the early work of Paul Tillich, partly because we will not be treating it again later and partly because its continuation of some of the main themes of liberal theology in a new, radical form will show most clearly how Karl Barth made a sharp break with this whole way of thinking.

Religious socialism made its first appearance among reforming pastors and labor leaders at the end of the nineteenth-century. While such movements were strictly controlled within the territory of the German Empire, religious socialism flourished in Switzerland before World War I, and indeed both Karl Barth and Emil Brunner worked with the religious socialists during their early careers as pastors.

Intellectual leadership for the movement, however, emerged in

Germany after the war, when socialists of all sorts who had been excluded from political power and academic influence found new opportunities to argue for fundamental political and economic changes. Paul Tillich, one of the most original and powerful thinkers in twentieth-century Protestantism, returned from service as a frontline chaplain to become a teacher of theology and a leader in the movement for religious socialism. His essays during the period from the fall of Imperial Germany to the rise of Adolf Hitler anticipate a sweeping restructuring of German industrial organization and the elimination of class structures that reflected existing economic inequities. It is striking, however, to note in his thought the persistence of the nineteenth-century theme of historical reconciliation of cultural and Christian values.[7]

Tillich expected that the vehicle for this reconciliation would be a religious form of socialism. Doubtless that struck many observers as an unlikely prospect. Workers in Europe were generally more conscious of social class differences than their American counterparts, and they took the repudiation of socialism by prominent religious leaders as an indication that Christianity was firmly bound to the interests of the capitalists. Moreover, religious socialists had to overcome the hostility to religion evident in the writings of Karl Marx, the founder of modern "scientific socialism."

Accordingly, Tillich began his most systematic work on Christian socialism by announcing that Christian socialists not only call people to a decision *for* socialism; they call, too, for a decision *about* it.[8] Religious socialism asks for adoption of a socialist program, but it also asks those who join that call not to interpret socialism in narrowly economic terms. What is needed is "a new vision of its nature, its problems, its difficulties, and its coming form."[9]

The new vision will be achieved, Tillich suggests, by looking behind the materialistic analysis of Marx to discover the understanding of history that drives the socialist movement and unites it with the biblical view of reality. The claim of Christian socialism is not that the Bible is socialist, but that socialism is in a profound sense biblical. The movement of history that led to the mood of prophetic expectation in the Old and New Testaments is repeated in the rising political expectations of the socialists.

What the biblical prophets and the modern-day socialists have in common is their rejection of all romantic urges to escape the tensions of the present by returning to the past. The glorification of the primitive German *Volk* and of German mythology by the Nazi movement exemplifies this romanticism and thus stands in fundamental opposition to the way of the prophets and the socialists. True religion does not look backwards. It anticipates a new social reality, and it allies itself with the movements that are working to bring it into being. At the same time, religion sustains these prophetic movements by showing how the concrete changes they propose are never complete in themselves, but always point beyond to a conclusion that transcends present conditions and cannot be fully accomplished by short-term programs or political successes.

The concept of prophetic expectation provides clear guidelines for Christians to join in action with the forward-looking socialists without simply losing their religious identity in the movement of political and economic history. Tillich also underscored the urgency of this cooperation in his discussion of the *kairos*,[10] the moment in history that affords an opportunity for decision between the romantic escape and the prophetic expectation.

Tillich clearly believed that the confusion and disorder of the postwar years offered such a *kairos* for religious socialism. Indeed, he and his associates in Berlin from 1919 to 1924 christened themselves the "Kairos Circle." Out of the confusions and oppositions of their time, they expected a synthesis that would unite socialism and "prophetism," overcoming the prevailing tensions between Christianity and socialism. The new socialism, with a clear awareness of its religious implications, would then be able to counter the growing tendency among the people to seek refuge from their problems in romantic nationalist movements.

The Socialist Decision, written in 1932, summarized a decade of this thinking. It was at once a call to action and a proclamation of the signs of the times. In Tillich's interpretation, socialism's rediscovery of its affinity with the prophets became the all but inevitable effect of the crisis of the 1920s. At the same time, this purified and clarified socialism was to assume into the synthesis the legimate concerns of its romantic opponents. The socialist decision was not only for those who advocate socialism but also for those "who today are its opponents, but who in the future will have to be its bearers."[11] Those who will be drawn with the inevitability of history to their proper place in the socialist synthesis include above all, as Tillich obliquely noted, "those groups that today carry the word *socialism* in their names." He meant principally, of course, the National Socialist German Workers Party, led by Adolf Hitler. The power of the *kairos* was such that even the Nazis might be led to a genuine socialist decision.

The course of subsequent events suggests that at the very least

10

Tillich's timing was off. As he wrote *The Socialist Decision* in 1932, the last cabinet of the Weimar Republic was faltering and Hitler was rising to power. Before the book could be distributed, it was suppressed by the new Nazi regime, and Tillich himself soon left Germany to teach in the United States.

Tillich's religious socialism was perhaps the most thoughtful continuation of German theology's search for a historical synthesis of religion and culture in the aftermath of World War I. Although his socialist views were politically radical, the stress on expectations rather than origins and the confident application of a historical dynamic that would resolve the apparently irreconcilable conflicts of the present mark a continuity in theological method between these early phases of Tillich's thought and that of his predecessors who shaped the liberal theological tradition at the University of Berlin. The failure of this liberal understanding of religion and culture, even in Tillich's reconstructed formulation, to provide the Christian community with an adequate understanding of events suggests the need for closer attention to alternatives to the search for historical synthesis.

Crisis Theology

While Tillich's account of Christian socialism continued some basic themes of nineteenth-century German theology, a quite different movement emerged in Switzerland. Karl Barth announced an interpretation of the Christian message that laid stress on the radical discontinuity between the truths of faith and human aspirations. Our progress is not merely interrupted by failures and miscalculations that keep us from reaching our highest goals; the goals themselves bespeak our refusal to acknowledge the sovereignty of God.

In response to the uncertainties of the time, Barth's theology was quickly dubbed the theology of crisis. Barth's intention, however, was not to offer a theological comment on the dislocations peculiar to postwar Europe. His point was that *all* times and cultures stand under the judgment of God, and against that standard, our relative human measures of good and evil make little difference.

Barth's rejection of the judgments that persons make in daily life imposes sharp limits on Christian participation in public moral choices, as we shall see in chapter 2. The key to Christian faith is the establishment of God's kingdom, and it is God, not we, who must inaugurate that kingdom and set the terms for its advance. The kingdom comes not by a convergence between Christian aspirations and human history, but as a judgment on history. So the practical wisdom that people

11

employ to shape events is irrelevant to faith. Its best achievements are not even a beginning for the work of God.

For the Christian, then, everything depends on God's commandments, and true wisdom begins with the understanding that God has the initiative in every action that is genuinely good. That means that human moral knowledge must be extremely limited. The moral rules we follow and the principles by which we distinguish good and evil are largely illusory, for we cannot limit God with our own crude generalizations. God's will for each situation is specific, and the human moral task is to hear it, not to arrive at our own judgments.

Barth's first account of God's judgment, then, reduces our moral choices to the single choice of obedience or rebellion. It silences our moral discourse by rendering our talk irrelevant to the real source of moral initiative. While Barth later recognized that this might leave us with too little guidance, he continued to insist on the freedom of God's action and to reject any generalizations that would tell us in advance what God will require of us.

For Barth's ethics, then, our moral expectations cannot be about what God will say, but only about where we are likely to hear it. The church as the community of those attentive to the Word of God and mindful of their history as God's covenant people becomes the important locus for moral discernment. The wider public discussion of moral issues must then be seen as a flawed attempt to speak about a good which, because it depends on the will of God, can be truly known only in the community of God's people. Christians may offer important guidance to the society as a whole, but they will not do that by participation in the general public discussion. They must witness to what they know in conscience before God without claiming that knowledge as their own possession or attempting to justify it in public terms.

Clearly, for such an ethics the significant society is the church, and Barth increasingly made the church the focus of his work. The importance of this change became apparent as German politics moved from the confusion of 1919 to the crude certainties of the Hitler era. Against pressures either to join forces with the Nazi movement or to form purely political alliances to resist it, Barth stood for the integrity of the Christian community. His work profoundly influenced those German Protestants who rejected Hitler's reach into the churches. Under Barth's theological guidance, they formed a "Confessing Church" to maintain their fidelity to the historic faith of the Reformation. The study of the beginnings of the Confessing Church which appears here in chapter 5 is thus an account of the public role of a church that refuses to participate in public moral discourse. Its witness to its own integrity and its demand for freedom to live out its own identity have important implications for the organization of the whole society even if the church is not concerned to make that case directly in a public forum. A church that understands its moral task in Barth's way does not stand in judgment on Nazism or any other ideology, but by being the church and by refusing to be anything else, it reveals God's judgment on the excessive claims of political leaders.

Readers who are chiefly interested in Barth's ethics may wish to read chapter 5 in close connection with chapter 2. A full understanding of Barth's work, however, requires attention to the theological controversies in which he participated. While formulating his sharp objections to movements that identified Christianity too simply with Nazism or democracy or socialism, he was also obliged to consider theological arguments for a more complex and cooperative relationship between Christian faith and public choices.

Theological Realism

Brunner and Bonhoeffer share Barth's insistence that the commandment of God is the starting point for Christian ethics. They, however, find that commandment embodied in the stable structures of human life, in the "orders of creation," as well as in the particular understandings of the Christian church. Because the family, government, economic life, and even the church itself have fundamental structures and patterns of authority that anyone can observe, the possibilities for general agreement on a course of action that corresponds to God's will are much greater than we might suppose. Diversity of beliefs about God need not prevent us from coming to agreement on action, and agreements on action that are framed by the requirements of these structures of human life may properly be regarded by Christians as the requirements of God's command. Of course, not every human agreement respects these structures. There are always persons who will contract to set aside the requirements of family life or social order for more immediate pleasures, and there are always leaders who will subordinate the legitimate needs of persons to their own political ambitions. Brunner and Bonhoeffer do not offer an unlimited validation of human choices, but they stress the general human capacity to recognize natural limits that determine whether our choices will work. Protestant ethics after World War I tended to neglect this natural

foundation for ethics. Bonhoeffer, especially, rediscovered its importance as he reflected on the destructive effects of Hitler's disregard for
natural limits.

The ethical theory which defines right actions as conformity to the
natural order is often called 'ethical naturalism'. Broadly understood,
that term applies to the work of Brunner and Bonhoeffer, but it is also
somewhat misleading. 'Naturalism' often connotes the reduction of
natural requirements to the simplest biological imperatives. It suggests
that the only appropriate question is what the organism requires to
survive and that any inquiry into more ultimate purposes in nature is
pointless. Clearly, neither Brunner nor Bonhoeffer was a naturalist in
that sense. Both insisted that the natural order derives its moral authority from God, not from biological necessity; and both recognized the
historical and cultural transformations that have modified the requirements of unadorned "nature."

Perhaps a better designation for the ethics of Brunner and Bonhoeffer would be 'realism'. Their American contemporaries, Reinhold
Niebuhr and John Bennett, used that term to emphasize that Christian
ethics cannot be just a pious recitation of religious ideals. It must come
to grips with the forces that oppose those ideals and limit their
achievement.[12] Brunner and Bonhoeffer are certainly realistic in this
common-sense way. They recognize that the command of God, however widely it may be known, will not be universally followed. More than
the American realists, however, Brunner and Bonhoeffer sought to
identify the ground for both the possibilities and the limitations in
God's will, which becomes visible in the structures of God's creation and
is available to guide anyone who has the wisdom to consult it. Moral
choice is neither the unlimited fulfillment of human wishes nor attentiveness to a word heard only by the faithful. It begins in our common
experience of human reality.

In these pages, the realist position is represented first by Emil Brunner, who shared Barth's awareness of a theological and social crisis but
who sought to define terms for Christian cooperation in the work of
reconstruction instead of emphasizing the distinctions between God's
kingdom and social reforms. In chapter 3 we will follow his treatment
of the "orders of creation" and their requirements in some detail.
While Brunner's specific recommendations will strike many readers
today as dated and rather conservative, his ethical method still has
much to teach us, for he describes a way that Christians can maintain
the sovereignty of God and still participate seriously in public moral

choices. He will not allow modern society to dismiss Christianity's hard-won insights into human experience as mere dogma with no general claim to truth, but neither will he permit Christians to avoid the strenuous requirements of social and scientific argument. A Christian engineer, Brunner remarks, "does not build 'Christian bridges' but solid bridges."[13]

Of course, Brunner was not the first to articulate this sort of realism in Christian ethics. In late antiquity, Jewish, Christian, and Stoic writers spoke of the "law of nature" known to all rational persons, which provides a fundamental guide to conduct that applies in all ages and cultures. This natural law became a basic element of Roman Catholic moral theology, and it gained new importance in modern times with the revival of Thomistic thought in the late nineteenth century. The polemical requirements of a preecumenical age obliged Brunner to stress the differences between his orders of creation and the natural law of the Catholic moralists, but an objective observer can hardly miss the similarities. In chapter 4 we will examine these in some detail, and we will see how on political questions, especially, Brunner came to rely increasingly on the traditions of natural law.

Bonhoeffer enters the discussion as a different, younger voice. He was still a student in secondary school when Barth's work began to appear, and he himself was educated in the great theological faculty at the University of Berlin, which took a dim view of these new developments in remote Switzerland. Bonhoeffer discovered, however, that Barth spoke to his own theological concerns more clearly than his teachers in Berlin, and, when the crisis of Hitler's rise to power overtook the churches, it was Barth who offered practical guidelines that seemed equal to the situation. The story of the Confessing Church in chapter 5 is Bonhoeffer's story as well as Barth's, for when the younger theologian took on the role of teacher and leader in the Confessing Church, the church he tried to create matched very closely the vision Barth articulated in the early 1930s.

The complications of subsequent history moved Bonhoeffer closer to Brunner's realism. By the time Bonhoeffer worked on his own *Ethics* (1940–43), he stressed the "rediscovery of the natural" and the importance of seeking God's commandment in the "divine mandates" of labor, family, government, and church—mandates which correspond closely to Brunner's orders of creation. In chapter 6 we will examine Bonhoeffer's role in the German resistance to Hitler, and we will see how those experiences led him to a new appreciation of Christian

15

cooperation in wider efforts to restore fundamental order to society. Bonhoeffer's realism, however, was never a simple endorsement of political action on secular principles. His theology demanded an awareness of God's presence in the history and social structures that everyone was trying to understand, so that reality includes the reality of God. Reality is not merely natural limits and human structures set in place by God; for Bonhoeffer reality includes Christ incarnate at a point in human history and Christ taking form in our history as a whole. Realism in Bonhoeffer becomes a distinctively theological realism. That is a qualification that Niebuhr or Brunner would no doubt have largely approved, but Bonhoeffer's achievement is also to show us, in theory and in action, one way that theological realism can be compatible with public moral choice.

Faith for a New Path

Barth, Brunner, and Bonhoeffer did not reach their conclusions on ethics all at once, nor do they offer us a single position that we can simply apply to our own problems. What they offer us are two quite different ways to proceed once we understand that Christian faith and the values of society generally are not simply identical. Barth's theology of crisis stresses the difference and calls Christians to give first attention to the Word of God and the integrity of the church. That theological preoccupation will have social consequences, and Barth is convinced that the results of this course will be better than any social change we might plan and initiate for its own sake. The theological realism of Bonhoeffer and Brunner always preserves the distinction between faith and culture, but it stresses the attempts to understand moral limits that link persons of faith to others in society and unites them in action against the many forces of modern life that treat the structures of family, culture, and government as though they could be disregarded in favor of more imperial ambitions.

Attention to these fundamental problems of faith and public choice gave Brunner, Barth, and Bonhoeffer a moral perspective broad enough to encompass the problems of Versailles, Weimar, and Hitler's Reich. It may also be broad enough to address some of the moral questions of our day, and chapter 7 indicates some of the ways in which contemporary Christian ethics continues the lines of crisis theology and theological realism laid down earlier in the century. Certainly that chapter is not a complete survey of Christian ethics, nor does it fully argue the case for theological realism, though the author's bias toward that position will by then be apparent. What the final chapter and this book as a whole do demonstrate, however, is that new questions in ethics can sometimes only be understood after looking more carefully at old ones.

NOTES

1. Jean Jacques Rousseau, *The Social Contract and Discourses,* trans. G. D. H. Cole (New York: E. P. Dutton, 1973), 174.

2. John Courtney Murray, *We Hold These Truths* (New York: Sheed & Ward, 1960), 28.

3. Karl Barth, *The Christian Life,* trans. Geoffrey W. Bromiley (Grand Rapids: Wm. B. Eerdmans, 1981), 69–70.

4. W. D. Ross, *The Right and the Good* (Oxford: At the Clarendon Press, 1930), 16–30.

5. Dietrich Bonhoeffer, *Ethics,* ed. Eberhard Bethge (New York: Macmillan Co., 1965), 272. Page references to Bonhoeffer's *Ethics* throughout this book are to the readily available paperback edition.

6. James Gustafson plays on this uneasy sense that we may have two quite different discussions of choice and conduct when he frames the title *Can Ethics Be Christian?* (Chicago: University of Chicago Press, 1975). Gustafson offers a cogent account of the points at which the two discussions interact. Bonhoeffer seems to formulate a sharper differentiation by titling one chapter of his *Ethics* "The 'Ethical' and the 'Christian' as a Theme." Clifford Green reports, however, that in Bonhoeffer's manuscript that title is followed by a question mark.

7. This brief study of Tillich's religious socialist writings cannot, unfortunately, trace the further development of his political ideas or do justice to the scope of his theological reflections. Readers interested in a more comprehensive historical survey of Tillich's ethics should see Ronald Stone, *Paul Tillich's Radical Social Thought* (Atlanta: John Knox Press, 1980).

8. Paul Tillich, *The Socialist Decision,* trans. Franklin Sherman (New York: Harper & Row, 1977), xxxi.

9. Ibid.

10. *Kairos,* a Greek word for time, takes on in biblical context the connotation of a decisive or opportune moment, the "acceptable year of the Lord" (Isa. 61:2), as opposed to *chronos,* time as a simple duration measured by clock or calendar.

11. Tillich, *Socialist Decision,* xxxi.

12. See Reinhold Niebuhr, *Christian Realism and Political Problems* (New York: Charles Scribner's Sons, 1953).

13. Emil Brunner, *The Divine Imperative,* trans. Olive Wyon (Philadelphia: Westminster Press, 1947), 263.

2
KARL BARTH:
THE ETHICS OF OBEDIENCE

Karl Barth made a sudden, striking appearance in the world of theology with the publication in 1921 of a second edition of his commentary *The Epistle to the Romans*. Barth had begun the commentary while a pastor in a small town in Switzerland, and he initially intended no more than to provide a resource for those who like himself had to preach biblical sermons to their congregations week by week. While he was revising *The Epistle to the Romans* for its second edition, however, he became convinced that a true theological response to the European situation would have to avoid all attempts at synthetic compromise with the distortions of the culture. The preacher must proclaim God's judgment not only against human wickedness, but against human righteousness as well. Armed with this conviction, Barth transformed Paul's moral exhortations into searing condemnations of those who claimed to know anything about the standards by which God judges human action.

> There is an obvious and important distinction between human unbelief and that faith which is also human. But these are superficial distinctions, which belong within the framework of this world. The veritable distinction between men and men, between the saved and the damned, between those who remain under the judgment of God and those who have been released from it, cannot be made according to a human standard.[1]

It is primarily this critical, negative element set against all the ordinary patterns of our thinking that leads us to call Barth's early theology dialectical.[2] Barth and his associates hoped that by establishing a genuine antithesis between Christian beliefs and the presuppositions of the culture they could avoid the easy synthesis that linked German Christianity after Schleiermacher to German nationalism and militarism.

Perhaps the more appropriate name for this first period in Barth's theology, however, is crisis theology. The name depends on a word play, for the German *Krise* and the English *crisis* both derive from the Greek *krisis,* which means *judgment.* Crisis theology looks beneath the defeats and commotions that occupy our attention and take the headlines in our newspapers to see the judgment of God on the events of history.

Human History and God's Judgment

What is it, then, that makes the historical crisis a genuine *krisis?* How do we begin to respond ethically to that judgment? What is it in our experience that alerts us to what God is doing?

Like Saint Paul, Barth found evidence of God's judgment in the phenomenon of *conscience.* In the early chapters of Romans, Paul explains that the Gentiles who violate God's commandments cannot make the excuse that they did not know what God requires. Even without the Jewish law, Paul insists, "they show that what the law requires is written on their hearts."[3] In the traditions of moral philosophy, Paul's reference to the "law written on the heart" provided a scriptural warrant for the idea of natural law. Barth, however, gives the theme of conscience a new twist. Conscience is the "perfect interpreter of life,"[4] but this does not make it an infallible guide to correct moral choice. What conscience correctly reminds us is that our human moral choice is one of corruption and confusion in the world. Instead of moral certainty, conscience introduces moral perplexity. The world is a place of ambiguity, arbitrariness, and contradiction, and conscience is the awareness that these realities persist in spite of our best efforts to tame them with moral rules or to ignore them in an irresponsible surrender to what the world asks of us. Conscience is not the assurance that I have done what I should; it is the nagging awareness that even after I have followed all rules, there is no goodness or righteousness in the world or in my life. Goodness and righteousness remain forever beyond my reach.

No doubt this experience of moral perplexity was in part a consequence of the war and the unprecedented new social situation that followed it. Wartime always strains ordinary moral rules to the breaking point, as violence and deceit become accepted tools of warfare and ordinary obligations to friends and family take second place to obligations to the nation.[5] After World War I, moreover, social relationships did not simply go back to normal. The end of the German Empire and a rising mistrust of traditional elites led to a breakdown of accepted social class lines. The deferential courtesies of lower ranks to higher, which had come to have an almost moral significance, began to disappear. The crisis Barth surveyed was a social crisis in all the ordinary senses of the term.

What gave the crisis theological meaning for Barth was his conviction that it is only in crisis that we truly experience God's relationship to our human world. In times of crisis, the inadequacy of every system that human beings have devised to govern themselves stands starkly revealed. While this crisis is not itself a revelation of God, it is perhaps more like the judgment of God than anything else in our human experience. Ordinarily, our life is a matter of making decisions about good and bad, making choices between plans that work and those that do not. Our everyday judgments as we read, write, buy, or vote are a sorting process; they bear little resemblance to the great judgment in which every plan we have to offer is rejected and all of our standards are thrown into confusion.

Barth finds a deliberate attempt to confound ordinary human judgment throughout Paul's letter to the Romans. The collapse of the distinction between Jacob and Esau, between Jew and Gentile reminds us of our own inability to sort the world neatly into the saved and the lost. Nor is it only in matters of religion that God's judgment undoes our human judging. God's judgment also shatters our conclusions about social programs, political parties, and popular culture. In the welter of conflicting movements that entered the scene after the First World War, Barth refused to choose a side. His relationship to the religious socialists weakened; he rejected the developments in contemporary philosophy; he refused to endorse nationalism or the League of Nations, capitalism or communism, reform or revolution. Precisely because God may establish a relationship with persons in any one of those positions, Barth insisted that one could not choose for or against them on the basis of faith.

That did not mean, however, that the positions were all equally good. It would be more to the point to say that all were equally bad, since none of them could provide the escape from ambiguity that they all promised. The European crisis becomes a *krisis,* the failure of our judging becomes the Judgment when we discern beneath the particular dislocations of the time the permanent jeopardy of the human situation. Underlying the failure of the German military or the Russian monarchy, the collapse of the Weimar Republic or of the New York Stock

Exchange, there was the radical contingency of the whole human situation. We can give reasons for doing this, that, or the other thing, but we can provide no justification for our own being.

Obviously, there can be no social solution to this human condition and no religious consolation for it either. "There is no escaping the problem of life, no hope of covering the conscience up and lulling it to sleep. There is no security here, not even religious security."[6] To be human is to live under judgment, in *krisis,* and our human crises only unmask the inadequacy of the schemes we employ to deny our vulnerability. Something quite different is required, something that would enable us to acknowledge what is happening without the pretense that we can understand or control it.

Barth's theological analysis of the postwar world differs sharply from Tillich's program which we examined in chapter 1. For Tillich, the bitter experiences of defeat and economic collapse could be turned to good use in human history. Seen through the eyes of prophetic faith, the crisis of the European order was a *kairos,* a time when history could be turned in a new direction, overcoming nostalgia for the past and accepting the demands of the future. Judgment occurs in history, and history provides the opportunity to move beyond it. Barth, by contrast, sees judgment as an interruption of human history and plans. Crisis occurs when we discover that reality cannot be controlled by our limited hopes and plans. Crisis becomes *krisis* when we understand at last that everything we do is called into question by a power totally outside of ourselves. The world which is a pleasant reflection of our own needs and goals is shattered, and that damage is beyond repair.

It may seem at this point that Barth has put an early end to this chapter, if not to this book. How can we proceed to talk about the making of theological ethics in the twentieth century if the truth of the matter is that every system of ethics is unmade before it is begun? Perhaps Barth means to leave us just where the existentialist philosophers do—in despair over the meaninglessness of every human enterprise, with only a courageous resolve to sustain us in the face of absurdity.

Surely that is where we would be, were it not for a strange duality in the shattering experience of judgment. What emerges in the *krisis* is not only the negation of every human attempt to explain, direct, and justify our lives, but also the paradoxical affirmation of our lives and action by a power outside of those rejected rules and inadequate systems. What is impossible is an ethics of rules, principles, and duties that tells us in advance what we ought to do. What is possible is an ethics of the Word of God.

The Word of God

It is not easy to say exactly what Barth means by the Word of God. Certainly he does not mean that we are to replace the systems of ethics and theology with a literalism that seeks divine commands directly from the pages of the Bible. The words of the Bible, no less than the words of the theologians and philosophers, are just that—words. Words become the Word only when they are transformed in experience by an encounter with the One who addresses us quite apart from our own explanations and self-justifications.

This is the positive side of that revelatory experience in which the historical crises of our time become for us the *krisis,* the judgment of God. At the same moment that we know we do not know what we ought to do, we hear the Word which tells us what to do. This experience of moral certainty apart from all systems is as real as the experience of the uncertainty of the systems. Indeed, Barth tells us, these are two aspects of the same experience.

An ethic of the Word of God thus avoids all claims to know or to state the principle by which a moral act can be identified. It insists that at moments of moral certainty, we are not dealing with a system of rules we could write out on paper and use to calculate our next moral move. We are confronted with a living God who addresses us and who refuses to be reduced to an object that our minds can easily grasp.

Now this insistence that God is always the subject who speaks *to us,* never an object we can investigate and analyze, runs consistently through the work of Barth and also through Brunner and Bonhoeffer. It established a limit within which theological ethics must work. The theologian who grounds ethics in our response to a God whose Word addresses us as a person addresses us can never reduce ethics to a human goal or a principle of action, as a philosopher seeking to make the moral life logically consistent might. There can be no slipping back into the old assumption that we have a system or a set of rules that will answer the question, What ought we to do? There must be no pretending that the great *krisis* has not happened; indeed the crises of history make that delusion impossible.

The theology Barth announced in *The Epistle to the Romans* became a rallying point for a new generation of theologians who rejected the union of theology and culture that had marked European Protestantism before the First World War. The popularity of *Romans* and

Barth's growing reputation as a teacher and lecturer drew attention to his ideas, but other voices joined the movement, too. In 1923, Barth and two of his associates, Eduard Thurneysen and Friedrich Gogarten, launched a new journal and gave it a name that expressed their own sense of the context of their work. Borrowing from the title of a paper by Gogarten, they christened their enterprise *Zwischen den Zeiten*, "Between the Times."[7]

Barth's early work thus establishes theological limits within which Christian ethics must work. Subsequent writers generally accepted those boundaries. They agreed that God's action somehow sets the stage for human moral life, and they, too, avoided ethical formulations that seemed to limit God's freedom and initiative. Some, however, argued that in preserving God's freedom Barth had also severely limited human thinking about action. Barth's critics complained that he had not shown that he could do the work of ethics within the limits of his theology of the Word of God. The yes in God's judgment might provide a momentary certainty about a particular moral action, but Barth's stress on the no seemed to preclude any attempt to speak about such moral convictions.

What the critics had in mind were passages like this one, from *The Epistle to the Romans:*

> Asceticism and movements of reform have their place as parables and as representations, but in themselves they are of no value. In no sense can they ever be even a first step towards the Kingdom of Heaven. There is but one good and one evil, one pure and one impure. Before God everything is impure; and therefore nothing is especially impure.[8]

Barth is insisting here that the task of ethics is simply to let the Word be the Word. Ethics must not try to speak for God. This reticence in the face of God's judgment is entirely appropriate to his theology, but it provides very little specific moral guidance. Barth's affirmation that the Word of God will be heard in life's critical moments provides a note of courage in the confrontation with massive evil, but the rules, systems, and principles which he rejects offer far more concrete guidance in ambiguous, everyday choices. Reinhold Niebuhr, who became one of Barth's most thoughtful critics in the United States, put it this way:

> Perhaps this theology is constructed too much for the great crises of history. . . . It can fight the devil if he shows both horns and both cloven feet. But it refuses to make discriminatory judgments about good and evil if the evil shows only one horn or the half of a cloven foot.[9]

Niebuhr poses a serious problem: If the theology of crisis provides more moral courage than moral guidance, Christian ethics may lose its role in helping persons to make particular, difficult decisions and may be unable to speak clearly on matters of public choice when different groups in the society come into conflict. Barth himself was disturbed by these criticisms, and even as he vigorously reasserted his theological interpretation of the European crisis, he sought ways to provide a basis for more definite prescriptions for action.

Ethical Generalizations

The critics' complaint seems to be that Barth's ethics lacks specificity. He speaks broadly of good and evil, but he refuses to identify the good and evil with something so particular as a defense policy or a welfare reform bill. He refuses to speak of evil in terms of petty promise breaking or marital infidelity.

It is clear, however, that Barth thinks the Word of God is specific. Particular human situations are not so small as to escape the judgment of God. The lack of specificity of which the critics complain is not because the Word of God is too general. Their complaint arises because Barth will not generalize about God's specific, particular Word. As individuals, we feel the impact of judgment on our actions. My lies, my petty cheating, stand condemned quite apart from all my perplexities about the wider social situation. Nevertheless, I cannot generalize the judgment on me to conclude that it falls equally on my neighbor's adultery or the office manager's deft withdrawals from the petty cash box.

By contrast, as we saw in chapter 1, generalizations about action are essential to public discussion of moral questions. To say that theft is morally wrong is more than a statement that I dislike theft. It implies that I have accepted or formulated for myself a rule concerning theft that applies to persons and their acts generally apart from what they (or I) happen to think. For Barth's critics who think in these terms, the lack of specificity in his ethics results, paradoxically, from his failure to generalize. Barth's insistence that God's judgment must not be limited and cannot be controlled makes it impossible to draw conclusions from any particular experience of judgment that might allow us to construct a systematic ethics.

The effort to build an ethics which begins with this common-sense notion that morality has something to do with knowing and following a set of rules comes to fullest expression in the works of Immanuel Kant (1724–1804). Barth recognized Kant as the originator of the ethical theory which had shaped his own education.[10] It will help us to grasp the uniqueness of Barth's position if we compare it briefly with the ethical systems inspired by Kant.

Kant begins his ethical investigations by noting that our moral approval seems to be directed toward a quality of the human will rather than toward the results of human action. Much as we appreciate the outcome when a peevish and self-centered millionaire saves a wooded hillside from destruction to preserve the view from his own mansion, we do not feel a moral approval for his act. What he did was entirely self-interested; any good that others derive from his "environmentalism" is irrelevant. Conversely, we do not blame the debtor who makes every effort to pay his obligations on time, only to be thwarted by a serious illness that deprives him of his income. We may insist that his legal obligation remains. We may even grumble that he should have taken out disability insurance, but our moral evaluation is a judgment about his intent, not an assessment of the results. To be sure, it is not always immediately clear that moral approval is directed toward the will and not toward its results, but Kant thought that this was due to the happy fact that a good will quite often produces generally satisfactory outcomes. If we will attend to the sort of examples I have suggested, however, Kant argues that we will see that "it is impossible to conceive anything at all in the world, or even out of it, which can be taken as good without qualification, except a good will."[11]

Kant proceeded to construct a systematic ethics on this basis by demonstrating that a good will is identifiable solely by its readiness to conform to a universal moral law. Any other basis simply confuses matters all over again, for if we select some particular good—such as happiness or justice or truthfulness—as the basis for our moral system, then we fall back at once into approving the *result*, and we lose the key insight that it is the will alone that can be morally good or evil.

Ethics in the Kantian tradition must rely heavily on the sort of generalization that Barth's theology will not permit. Since no attention to results or circumstances will enable us to evaluate an action morally, we must ask instead whether there is a general rule, a "categorical imperative" in Kant's terms, that would dictate the action in question. Such a rule would be one that any rational being could agree to follow, even without knowing the results, but always remembering that others will be obliged to follow the same rule. It is difficult to know precisely what rules might meet the test, but it is fairly clear that a maxim like "Lie your way out of any situation when your finances are at stake"

NC WESLEYAN COLLEGE
ELIZABETH BRASWELL PEARSALL LIBRARY

would fail. "Always attempt to do what you have promised," by contrast, would be more likely to succeed.[12]

The Kantian ethic, which was very much a part of Barth's intellectual background, is thus an ethic of duty and one that relies on general moral rules. The technical name for such a system is *rule-deontology* (from the Greek *deon*, or duty). A rule-deontology emphasizes the importance of obedience to moral imperatives even when the situation seems to allow other actions that would produce better results or when the immediate results of following the rules seem to be undesirable. The imperatives to be obeyed, in turn, can be stated in the form of general rules that apply to everyone's conduct.

The Kantian emphasis on obedience was congenial to Barth, but the emphasis on general rules was not. Barth stresses the specificity of the Word of God to every human situation. He insists that rules or generalizations cannot encompass all that God's judgment may be saying and cannot predict in advance what that judgment will be. The effect of Barth's stress on the Word of God is to call all rules into question and to focus our attention back on the unique act.

As a critic of Kant, of course, Barth was not alone. Almost from the first appearance of Kant's systematic ethics, other authors had denied his sharp distinction between moral approval and the approval of results. Kant was simply mistaken, the theorists of this opinion argued. Moral action always has to do with bringing about certain sorts of results.

Philosophers today call an ethics which takes this approach a *teleology* (from the Greek *telos*, or goal). Of course, there have been many opinions about precisely what this goal of moral action is. Jeremy Bentham, Kant's English contemporary, insisted that it was simply general human happiness, and English and American utilitarians have tended to follow his view. German theorists, by contrast, were more likely to specify some ideal form of human life—Nietzsche's "superman," for example—or to prescribe a specific set of values that human moral action is to bring into being. Barth's contemporary, Max Scheler (1874–1928) drew on Roman Catholic sources to create an anti-Kantian ethic based on the realization of specific values in human life.

A *rule-teleology* directs persons in the pursuit of these goals through a system of rules. Moral rules decide specific cases, but the task of ethics is to determine which rules would on the whole produce the best results. A more thoroughgoing application of the goal-seeking principle is *act-teleology*, a moral system which, like Barth's ethics, focuses on the

NC WESLEYAN COLLEGE
ELIZABETH BRASWELL PEARSALL LIBRARY

possibilities and limits of the specific situation and makes a choice without the guidance of general rules. What neither act- nor rule-teleologists supply is the strong emphasis on the moral value of obedience that characterizes Barth and Kant alike. In a teleological ethics the goal, rather than the rule, provides the generalization and is the proper object of moral respect. Teleological ethics cannot evaluate all situations in terms of basic moral rules that apply to everyone, but it begins moral reflection with the general observation that all persons seek certain experiences of pleasure, love, or happiness. Or it may argue that all persons ought to acquire certain virtues like generosity, courage, or wisdom. To decide about telling the truth or keeping a promise, the teleologist focuses on the human happiness or the specific virtue that this action should enhance. Inevitably, this leaves a somewhat wider scope for individual decision and evaluation than a strict deontology would allow. Whether I should keep a promise may turn on an assessment of how much happiness or misery keeping it will create. Whether I may lie in a complex, problematic situation will depend on an assessment of the long-term consequences of truth or falsehood.

Clearly, then, a teleological ethics cannot provide the alternative to Kantian rule-deontology which Barth was seeking. The reliance on prediction and calculation, either for immediate decisions or for social rules, is hardly suited to a time of crisis, when the stabilities that allow such precise determinations are all called into question. More important, the attempt to establish goals that would be relevant to every human situation of choice strikes Barth as equally fruitless with the search for general moral rules, and equally heedless of the judgment of God on all our expectations. If Barth will not allow us to take refuge in the security of universal rules, he most certainly will not allow us the security of results.

Barth thus rejects not only the Kantian form of the ethic of duty; he rejects the major teleological alternatives as well. The type of ethic he endorses can only be described as an *act-deontology*.[13] Barth's ethics includes a duty which demands obedience regardless of results, but, unlike Kant, Barth insists that the duty can only be known as a requirement to do a specific deed in a specific situation. Duty can never be found in a general rule.

Where then do we find the point of generalization that systematic ethical reflection seems to require? Neither the rule of action nor the action's goal provides this for Barth. The only possible source of generalization is the command itself. An ethic of the Word of God affirms that what God commands in the situation is right. Barth's deontology can make few general statements beyond that. Certainly it cannot accept any generalizations that allow us to predict what God will command or that set an independent standard of right to which God's command must conform. We may indeed affirm in prayer and liturgy that God always commands us to do the loving thing, but the act-deontologist will insist that we make that generalization *only* if we mean that whatever God commands is what it means for us to love. If we think we can predict God's command by reflecting on our own experience of loving, we have deluded ourselves and slipped back into an act-teleology that is searching for a human experience rather than listening for the Word of God.[14]

Preserving the Freedom of God

Barth's act-deontology is not without philosophical parallels. The legal philosophy of positivism, for example, asserts that valid laws cannot be identified by their logical form or by their moral content. Valid law, according to the positivists, is simply law issued by someone who has the authority to make law. Wise regulations proposed by citizens' committees are not law; foolish measures passed by legislatures are, and that is all that can be said on the matter.

Barth's position, however, is slightly different.[15] Whereas a legal positivist assumes that those who have no authority to make law may nonetheless have the wisdom and experience to criticize it, the ethic of the Word of God begins with the assumption that the meaning and purpose in God's action are forever beyond human evaluation. Neither rules nor goals are proper points for generalization in ethics, because neither can comprehend the divine action with which all true ethics begins. God takes the initiative to make his will known in judgment on the prevailing human situation. The appropriate ethical response for those who hear the Word is not deliberation but obedience.

This radical challenge to the usual conceptions of ethics is precisely what we should expect from an ethic that begins with the experience of crisis. It is not only our rules, evaluations, and moral certainties that collapse under the judgment. The idea of ethics itself must be changed. The confusion of conscience which we meet whenever we reflect clearly and honestly on contemporary moral experience will not, Barth insists, resolve itself on its own. Certainty can only be found again in a directive that originates outside of us; indeed, that is where certainty has been from the beginning. What the final *krisis* of divine judgment portends does not begin in historical crisis, but crisis helps make the meaning of judgment clear to us. Where the German people sought strength and security, they found weakness and defeat. Where the theologians sought God, they found only a magnified image of themselves. Where moral men and women sought certainty and confidence, they found only confusion and doubt. There is no way to set these activities right again. The proper response is to turn from them to a new center of activity, to God, who enters our human situation with a judgment that creates our confusions and that will also resolve them, if only we will learn that his freedom cannot be bound by our systems.

Barth recognizes, of course, that ethics in the traditional sense, deliberation about right and wrong and the setting of human moral standards, will go on. In *The Epistle to the Romans*, he treats Paul's discussion of the strong and the weak[16] as a recognition that we will always have to deal with human systems and the judgments they imply. The early Christians could not escape controversies over food and drink and sacred observances, even though Paul understood that such regulations had been decisively surpassed. So, too, Barth insists that an ethic of the Word of God surpasses the most pressing issues of ordinary ethics and renders them unimportant. That message is repeated again near the end of *The Epistle to the Romans*.

> All is subject to the judgment of God. *Judge not* is therefore the only possibility. And yet, even this possibility is no possibility, no recipe; it provides no standard of conduct. We have no alternative but to range ourselves under the judgment that awaits us, hoping—without any ground for our hope—for the impossible possibility of the mercy of God.[17]

Despite this negative result for ethics, we cannot but be impressed with the theological significance of Barth's early work. As he overthrows all the systems and programs in which his contemporaries had placed their confidence, he also recovers the basic meaning of a genuine encounter with God. "Judge not, that you be not judged" is more than a moralistic slogan. It is addressed to a believer who stands in a personal relationship to God, who reserves the right of judgment. The commandment "Judge not" is not an admonition to be kind to your neighbor or a call for broad-minded tolerance regarding the behavior of others. It is first a reminder not to turn the Other who addresses us as judge into an object. We are to refrain from judging the neighbor because such judgment is a sign that we think we have also mastered God.

God is always the active subject in moral action, never an object of our moral knowledge. God's freedom and initiative must be preserved. These are fundamental limits in Barth's theology, and he will maintain them even if it means the end of theological ethics in any conventional sense. If the problem of ethics is to provide a secure universal standard by which we can judge the actions of others, Barth will insist that the problem cannot be solved.

The problem of ethics, however, is not only that I want to judge my neighbor. That temptation may be resisted, but I still have a need to evaluate myself; and even if I am quite certain that I know my duty in this situation, I may want to explain my choice to someone else. Barth's act-deontology leaves little scope for such efforts because the ethic of the Word of God demands relentless attention to a divine activity that always transcends my awareness and escapes my full comprehension. The original action in all genuine ethics is God's action. While I can experience a certainty about God's commandment in obedient action, I cannot speak of it with the same assurance.

The key to a restoration of theological ethics as a human activity, therefore, must be a way of speaking about God that does not reduce him to a divine object or to a procedure in some method for making moral judgments. At the same time that Barth was defending his ethic of the Word of God, he was seeking a way to speak of it with more specificity and certainty.

From Dialectics to Analogy

To speak of God without making God into just another object may seem a peculiarly tricky theological task, but it is actually not so different from a challenge that everyone faces everyday. Every person we meet has to be treated as an independent center of action and initiative. Traffic police, economic analysts, and behavior modification therapists may be able to treat human beings like complex, preprogrammed automatons; but in most of our relationships we are obliged to remember that these others with whom we deal are themselves subjects not just objects for our manipulation. We can never know what goes on in another person's mind, but we always suppose that another person's consciousness is basically like our own. To guess what another is thinking or to say, "I understand how you feel" is not so much a matter of knowing as it is the result of a complex process of *analogy* by which we infer things about another person's ideas or emotions from the structures of our own.

This everyday way of thinking also has a history as a theological method, for theologians have long suggested that reliable ideas about God, whom we cannot know directly, can be formed by analogy with what we do know about his creatures. What we can say about God with certainty, these theologians suggest, we say because we assume that the structure of his being is reflected in the world he has made. While our thoughts are not God's thoughts, as Isaiah warns, still God's thoughts are enough like our own that something can be learned of God from attention to our human experience.

Because the whole history of Christian theology offers really rather few ways to speak directly about God, we should not be surprised that Barth eventually turned to the method of analogy in an effort to make his ethics more specific. Because of what we have seen thus far of Barth, we should not be surprised to learn that he also turned the method on its head.

The change in Barth's theological method coincided with important changes in his own life and work. He left Switzerland and his parish ministry and began a teaching career in Germany, where he joined the theological faculty at the University of Göttingen. The demands of regular lecturing proved quite different from the demands of preaching and pastoral care, and Barth paints an amusing picture of himself in this period, sitting up late at night with his cigars, poring over Calvin's *Institutes* in a frantic effort to stay one step ahead of his students.

Barth was perhaps not quite so unprepared as he felt, but there is no doubt that the new university setting expanded his intellectual horizons. For the first time, he had an opportunity for serious dialogue with Roman Catholic theologians, and the basic works of Catholic theology occupied an important place in his studies during the mid-1920s. The professor of Reformed theology, who had dismissed the systems of Thomism as sophisticated attempts to objectify God, developed a new appreciation of the pre-Reformation heritage he shared with his Roman Catholic counterparts. Medieval theology was more than an elaborate exercise of pride in human reason. It was in Anselm's phrase, *"fides quarens intellectum,"* faith seeking understanding.[18]

These new interests are perhaps most apparent in Barth's writings on ethics. He was obliged to lecture extensively on the subject in 1928 and 1929, first at the University of Münster and then in Bonn, and it was just at this time that he had entered public discussions with the noted Catholic theologian Eric Przywara, S.J. Barth was attempting to clarify his position in ethics, drawing more extensively on traditional materials to refute the charge that his work lacked specificity. At the same time, he had to answer a new group of critics who complained that Barth was becoming a Catholic! Clearly this work on ethics would have to walk a theoretical tightrope.

Despite these pressures, or perhaps because of them, Barth was able to formulate a new position in ethics that he retained for the rest of his career. The lectures of 1928–29 set the ethical themes that run throughout the massive *Church Dogmatics*.[19] To explore these mature works in detail would require a book in itself, but the important point for the present is to understand Barth's new attempt to speak definitively about God's action.

We have already suggested how a sort of analogical thinking enables us to understand the thought and actions of other persons. We think this way so constantly that it is startling to reflect that the object we are thinking about, the consciousness of another person, never is a part of our own experience. Analogy allows us to speak decisively about something we cannot actually know, and we all rely on our analogical generalizations to guide us in our dealings with others. Every time we say, "I know how he thinks" and go on to plan our actions according to the predictable responses of an employer, spouse, or professor, we quietly acknowledge that we know some things we cannot touch or measure and that the general conclusions we draw from this knowledge are reliable guides to action. At the same time it is only the analogy that assures us that this other person is a free consciousness with a mind of his or her own. Far from binding the other's freedom in rigid expectations, analogical thinking provides the only way we have to understand another's freedom in the first place.

In Catholic theology, this way of thinking became a theological method with wide applications.[20] It allowed inferences not only from human personality and activity to God's freedom and agency, but also from the order of things in the world to God's purposes in creation. Since we can conceive God as an active being with intentions and purposes, the underlying argument ran, we can also use the same analogical method to discern what those purposes are, drawing conclusions from the way things work together in the world of our experience. What is true about us, made in God's image, may be true of God as well. The order of the world may tell us something about the eternal order which is the mind of God.

The "analogy of being" (*analogia entis*) lends a measure of confidence to our theological assertions. Analogy, of course, is not identity, and theologians stress that every statement about God based on an analogy to our human experience is also implicitly a statement about how God *differs* from our humanity. Nevertheless, analogical arguments provide a reasonable basis for trusting our considered statements about what God is doing and about God's intentions for human creatures. Certainly the *analogia entis* seems to be an alternative to Barth's early insistence that God escapes all our categories. The argument by analogy reminds us that what is not directly experienced need not be utterly unknown.

But does the analogy reach far enough to touch the reality of God? Much as Barth was attracted to the systematic and self-assured theology of his Catholic colleagues, he quickly saw that it turned on an unspoken premise—a premise that his Protestant theology had to question.

Analogical reasoning works in human relationships because we have some experience of human reality. We can say, "I know what he's thinking" because we do know in general terms how a human being thinks, and we have clues from ordinary experience, extended conversations, and even from brain research that the other persons we encounter are put together in ways that enable them to think as we do. If, however, we notice the family dog eyeing our dinner steaks and say, "I know what he's thinking," the analogy is much less precise. What is a dog thinking? *Does* a dog think? Does a preverbal infant think? Does one need a brain to think, and if so does *God* think? Analogical thinking may extend our knowledge beyond direct experiences, but it clearly works best when there is a strong base of experience on which to build.

The question Barth confronted was precisely whether there is such a base of experience when we come to talk about God. The *analogia entis* presupposes that ordinary human experience includes not only the evidence of God's work, but some awareness of God as the fundamental reality behind all particular experiences. To be sure, Catholic theologians have warned that this awareness is limited. It needs to be instructed by teachings of the church, extended by theological argument, and tested by Scripture. Nevertheless, the basis for the analogy is there. "For all that may be known of God by men lies plain before their eyes; indeed God himself has disclosed it to them. His invisible attributes, that is to say his everlasting power and deity, have been visible, ever since the world began, to the eye of reason in the things he has made."[21]

Protestant theology by contrast has stressed the limitations that sin imposes on human reason and the fundamental distortions of our experience that result from our separation from God. While many authors of the Reformation conceded that sinful reason retains a capacity to understand and order human affairs, they were equally insistent that such reason can know nothing of God. On that point Calvin says, "the greatest geniuses are blinder than moles!"[22] In sinful human beings the preliminary awareness of God that would allow the analogical investigation to begin is missing or obscured.

Barth always defended this Protestant position in its strongest form. Indeed, we shall see in the next chapter that his insistence on this point finally separated him from some Reformed theologians who had supported his early work. The insistence that God is always subject, never an object for our knowing, that God is available to us in act only, means in part that God is less available to our analogical knowledge than our human neighbors are. What we have of God is only what God gives us immediately, not the objectified God that theologians distill from human experience; and without that which God gives us, our analogical attempts to speak of God have nowhere to begin and nothing significant to say. Apart from God's active self-revelation, analogical theology is, as Barth says, like an argument between bats and moles about the nature of the sun.[23]

Thus the problem: Barth's ethics needs the measured certainty that analogical reasoning provides, but Barth's theology precludes a direct adoption of the methods he discovered in pre-Reformation writers. The solution he proposed was to place his confidence in God's self-revelation and begin the analogy there, so that the end point of the medieval reasoning became Barth's starting point, while the human world is known by analogy to what we know of God. In place of the *analogia entis,* which reasons from the world to God, we have an *analogia fidei* (analogy of faith), which reasons from God to permanent and reliable truths about humanity.

This theological method is not easy to understand, but because it dominates Barth's later work, it will be worthwhile to study it in detail to decide whether it solves the ethical problems that we found in *The Epistle to the Romans.* We might choose any one of many passages from the *Church Dogmatics* for this purpose, but it will be convenient here to examine a single lecture, *The Holy Ghost and the Christian Life,* which Barth delivered in October 1929.[24]

Part of the meaning of the *analogia fidei* is immediately apparent in the structure of the lecture, which is divided into three sections—the Holy Ghost as creator, the Holy Ghost as reconciler, and the Holy

Ghost as redeemer. Clearly, Barth does not intend to describe the work of the Spirit in ways that separate this person of the Trinity from the rest of God's activity. A lecture which spoke chiefly about a comforting sense of God's presence or which emphasized special religious experiences could not be an adequate presentation of the Holy Ghost and the Christian life. Rather, the Spirit is present in all that God does, and everything that God does becomes present to us through the Spirit. Our place in God's creation and Christ's death on our behalf are works of the Spirit that shape our lives, quite as much as the charismatic events that are sometimes specially labeled "works of the Spirit." The structure of the Trinity becomes the key to understanding God and, ultimately, to understanding ourselves.

The same point explains Barth's insistence that Christ must be the focus of the *analogia fidei*. If this is taken to mean a special interest in the life and ministry of Jesus, the point is lost. The loving and compassionate character of Jesus is important only when we see it as a revelation of God's creative intention toward us, while talk about a loving and compassionate Creator is meaningless unless the Spirit makes it real in our own experience. Whatever we can know about God must be given in the threefold structure of his revelation to us. Anything we attempt to say apart from that revelation will be incomplete and distorted. A discussion that speaks only of the Father or the Son or the Spirit conveys at best a partial truth no matter how carefully it is devised. A theology that subordinates two Persons of the Trinity to a third, or collapses the differentiation between Father, Son, and Spirit into a premature unity cannot be a Christian theology at all. It may repeat the human striving toward God that characterized the *analogia entis,* but it forsakes God's reach toward humanity that is the basis for an *analogia fidei.*

Thus the doctrine of the Trinity becomes the interpretative key for Barth's new analogical theology. Far from being a symbol by which the church speaks of what cannot be said, the doctrine of the Trinity is a concrete guide to what can and must be said about God. It warns us that no single statement about God can be complete in itself, but it also insists that our statements taken together must form a certain unity. What we have to say about God is more than a collection of teasing paradoxes and illuminating contradictions. What we have to say about God must point to divine activity along three quite specific dimensions: creation, reconciliation, and redemption.

The trinitarian structure demanded by the *analogia fidei* provides a perspectival approach to truth that was impossible in the pure dialectic of Barth's early work. There the Word of God could be heard only as the singular shattering truth that silenced all other voices by revealing their confusion. Here the Word can appear whole only when the truth of creation is modified by the truth of reconciliation, and both again are interpreted through the truth of redemption. The dialectical insistence that God has a unique Word for each situation yields now to a recognition that the Word can never be understood all at once. The complexity of our hearing must match the complexity of God's being. That is the basic idea of the *analogia fidei*.

Since the trinitarian principle of interpretation reminds us constantly that everything we try to say about God is incomplete and partial, Barth might be able to resolve some of his problems in ethics by recognizing the partial truth present in ideas that he previously rejected. Something like that seems to happen in *The Holy Ghost and the Christian Life*, as Barth reintroduces some basic concepts from previous systems of Christian ethics.

Conscience, for example, no longer has the negative role as witness to human corruption and moral confusion. It recovers a positive place in the moral life as one of the signs of the presence of the Redeemer.[25] (Other signs Barth mentions are gratitude and prayer.) Conscience resumes its classic function as *con-scientia*, a "co-knowledge" with God about what is good and evil. The presence of God as redeemer seems to imply, after all, that we can have some reliable moral knowledge.

Of course, Barth does not want us to take this co-knowledge in its most literal sense, as though good and evil were things that exist apart from God, objects that God and I both know, like you and your neighbor both know the same trees on the block or the location of the corner mailbox. Some of Barth's Catholic contemporaries, notably Max Scheler, spoke of an objective order of values that really exists in the world as a foundation for ethics,[26] but Barth clearly did not want his *analogia fidei* confused with that.

Good and evil for Barth still begin and end in the will of God. While Barth is open to dialogue and argument about how we know the will of God or over what, precisely, the will of God is, he never moves from the fundamental position that the meaning of 'good' can only be established by the will of God. Philosophers call this inquiry into what moral terms mean 'metaethics' in order to distinguish it from ordinary ethical questions about which things are good or which acts are right.[27] Questions of ordinary or 'normative' ethics are questions about whether the things we call right or good really are so. It seems at first that two persons might disagree strongly about a normative decision over, say, whether it is right to pay taxes to support an unjust war, and yet they might agree on the metaethical point that being right can only mean that God wills that action. Normative disagreements do not imply metaethical disagreement, nor does metaethical agreement imply that the parties will automatically agree on the normative question of what it is right to do. Or so most writers suggest. The unique point in Barth's ethics is his insistence that once we are clear about the fundamental metaethical question, the answers to the normative questions will quickly fall into place. Because God's will is something we can never control or predict, the only way we can know what is good or right is to hear the Word. When we are clear that 'good' and 'right' can have no meaning apart from God's specific will for each situation, we will cease looking elsewhere for clues to what we ought to do.

Nevertheless, in the constancy of God's presence for us as reconciler, we recognize a persistent intention for us in creation, and in God's presence as redeemer we are restored to a place of responsibility in that creation. In the midst of a disordered life, we begin to see the regularities God intended. Marriage, the state, the ethnic community, and the community of faith—all of these, Barth finds, have a stable place in God's intention. They are not passing commands to suit the moment; they reappear in various civilizations and ages of history with a regularity which any objective student of human society can see. Persons are constituted physically and psychologically so that they require a certain order of things to survive and thrive. Any careful observer can discern these requirements; a faithful observer also recognizes in them the commands of God the Creator.

Barth here touches on a theme that we will encounter repeatedly in Protestant writers during this period. Barth, Brunner, and Friedrich Gogarten all spoke of these "orders of creation,"[28] though Barth's use of the term is confined to his lectures in the late 1920s. He sometimes speaks, not of the orders, but more generally of the "autonomy" or self-regulation of creation,[29] and he completely abandons the language of the orders after pro-Nazi theologians began to employ it for their own purposes.

The hesitation over the idea of "orders of creation" is understandable. It implies a rather fixed, static social system, and all of these theologians felt keenly the changes and unpredictability that World War I had imposed. Nevertheless, they could not deny that even in social chaos some human relationships seemed to be constant. People continued to marry and form families. They sought a livelihood and leisure, and they turned to various forms of worship. If little was certain in the events of the day, still some human aspirations were predictable, and these could perhaps be the basis for definitive moral requirements. If childrearing seems to require firm paternal authority and regular maternal attention (as most of these writers would have said it does), then may we not say that at least some elements of the traditional family structures are *required* by the command of the Creator? If persons in all societies and civilizations try to express a basic sense of reverence in worship, may we not conclude that the order of creation places religion in its own essential position, not dependent on the power of the state?

Needless to say, many critics today would argue that these writers moved too quickly from the traditions of their European society to the permanent requirements of the human condition. For the moment, however, we are less concerned with their conclusions than with the pattern of reasoning they used. Is it possible to move in thought from the apparent requirements of natural and social order to conclusions about God's intentions and divine commandments?

Such reasoning strains the *analogia fidei,* perhaps to the breaking point. It proceeds from a single point in revelation, the knowledge that the world depends finally on God's will and power and then argues that God's persistent intention can be seen in the consistent workings of the world. The argument stops short of the *analogia entis,* which would suggest that even the divine reality of God can be inferred from the facts of nature, but the line between the two analogies is at this point very thin indeed.

The Protestant writers who spoke of the "orders of creation" or in similar terms were aware of the problem, but the need for a stable, knowable foundation for moral argument was so great that Brunner chose to adopt the idea. Bonhoeffer would use the concept of "divine mandates" in a similar way during the dislocations of World War II. Barth hesitated, then concluded that this idea of orders of creation contains a dangerous tendency that is incompatible with his main theological idea. The autonomy of the world is merely apparent, Barth suggests. To be sure, the world goes its way in certain predictable patterns, but we do not understand this properly unless we understand them in radical dependence on God. The orders of creation cannot be independent ways of knowing God; they must be ways that God has of relating to us.

> If the creature is to be strictly understood as a reality willed and placed by God in distinction from His own reality; that is to say, as the wonder of a reality, which, by the power of God's love, has a place and persistence alongside of His own reality, then the continuity between Him and it (the true *analogia entis,* by virtue of which He, the uncreated Spirit, can be revealed to the created spirit)—this continuity cannot belong to the creature itself, but only to the Creator *in His relation* to the creature.[30]

Barth sometimes calls this "true *analogia entis*" an "*analogia relationis.*" He means always to distinguish his analogy, under whatever name, from the traditional *analogia entis,* which takes our knowledge of the world as a secure starting point for thinking about God. There is no way to reason from facts about the world to the will of God. The only valid line of argument runs in the opposite direction.

Barth suggests that the problem with the *analogia entis,* indeed, the problem with any form of natural law or ethics based on scientific fact, is that we cannot turn our knowledge of things into specific guidelines for our own conduct.[31] A generalization about the way the world is shares the problem of the moral generalizations that he had once criticized in *The Epistle to the Romans.* "These 'orders' were laid down by God at the creation, and even now they are directions intended for my living. But what, for example, work, marriage, family, etc., signify just now in my particular case, as God's 'orders', I do not know."[32] As general accounts of human experience, the orders of creation have a certain validity. Their place in Christian thought may, indeed, be enhanced by discoveries in psychology, sociology, or political science. Nonetheless, no general truth in science or in ethics can provide the certainty that would resolve our doubts and end our confusion about what we are to do. That assurance comes only from hearing the Word of God.

Barth's analogical method thus retains his first insistence that our human knowledge cannot give us a claim on God. To suggest that God's commandments must comply with the orders we know in nature or in human society would limit God's freedom to act and to establish relationships with us at will, and so we must abandon that claim for theological reasons. This restriction, however, severely curtails the effort to build an ethic that would include the responsibility for creation which is restored to us in our relationship to God as reconciler. To be sure, the dialectical method is somewhat softened. God's command is not arbitrary, a momentary expression of divine will unrelated to anything else in creation. What the Word commands will be related to God's persistent purposes in creation and redemption. However, the command itself is something I can receive only in an *action* of God. It is part of God's presence to me as a subject. The commandment never becomes an object which I can possess for later reflection or which I could demonstrate to the satisfaction of those who doubt it.

So, no less than in the dialectical method of *The Epistle to the Romans,* the theological imperative to preserve God's freedom and initiative appears to rule out the predictability and universality that systematic thinking in ethics requires. Perhaps no act-deontology based on divine command can avoid this dilemma. We might, if we believed in a once-and-for-all revelation recorded in the Bible or concentrated in the Ten Commandments, establish a permanent record of God's requirements, but Barth believes in a living God whose commandments must be sought in a Word for us today. The words of the Bible may become that Word for us, but they can never capture the Word and hold it for us to examine as we wish. The freedom and initiative of God means that God has the initiative in moral action, too; we can only respond in obedience when we know *now* what God requires.

What, then, do we gain for ethics in the methodological shift from dialectics to analogy? The results are not negligible, for analogy permits us to understand what it would mean to be redeemed from the *krisis* that the dialectic forces upon our attention.

Redemption occurs when the troubled conscience that is under judgment becomes a genuine *con-scientia,* a knowing with God. When we respond in obedience to the Word of God, the confusion imposed by conflicting human laws and theories disappears, and we know clearly what we are required to do. More than that, we know our own action in continuity with God's persistent intentions for the world. Obedient action is more than a momentary response to a single command, it is a pattern of living responsibly within the order which God is creating in the human world. The redeemed, obedient conscience knows itself at one with the intentions of God. The uncertainty and anxiety of the crisis subside, and life goes forward in response to an initiative from beyond our limited, human purposes.

The reconciled and redeemed conscience knows with God, but it cannot know that it knows. Any break in the immediacy of obedience, any attempt to say, "Now I know what it is," severs the relationship to God and turns us back in upon ourselves. The presence of the Holy Spirit in our lives, Barth says at one point, is *eschatological,* never *ontological.*[33] He means that we can never treat God's presence as a fact about ourselves. We can only receive it as a promise in our actions.

Where, then, does this *analogia fidei* leave us in our investigation into ethics? Barth has found a place in God's plan for responsible action.

Everything we do is not so pointless and self-deceiving as the dialectic seemed to imply. Now the loving marriage, the responsible government, and the faithful congregation serve some purpose in the order of things; but when we seek to identify what makes a marriage loving, a government responsible, or a congregation faithful, we are where we were. The child of God knows in action what God's will requires, but this certainty is neither visible to his neighbor nor available for his own reflection.

> He may be such a one, of course, that has maxims, at least to outward view—("to the pure all things are pure")—he may be a realist or an idealist; these principles of his may be conservative or revolutionary: he may be a Pietist, perhaps, but quite as well a Communist. . . . Who is this child? Who is there that has such a good and honest conscience? Is it thou or I; this man or that? I have not said so. Had I done so I would have been teaching in the Augustinian style and denying the promise as promise.[34]

The ethic of the *analogia fidei,* no less than the ethic of the dialectic, leaves us with that problem of which Niebuhr complained. It can identify the devil, but it can do little else.

Barth might protest that his ethic does at least one important thing more. It warns us pointedly not to deify our own choices, for the price of that idolatry is that we cut ourselves off from ever hearing the demand that genuinely comes from beyond ourselves.

> Actual hearing, a hearing that actually makes us conscious of another than ourselves—a hearing that gives us one really opposite to us—can, indeed, be only the hearing of the Word of God. In the case of any other hearing, in the end we hear only the echo of our own voice, in unbounded solitariness.[35]

Nevertheless, our specific choices, as long as we do not treat them as ultimate, remain curiously beyond the reach of human judgment. My choice of a political party, my neighbor's advocacy of some new public policy, the style of family life I want, and also the sort of family my spouse wants to have—all of these may be responsible choices based on the command of God. May be—or may not.

The problem with Barth's eschatological redemption is that it gives us no specific ethical guidance for choices in the present. Barth warns us not to deify our own preferences, as if they were the Word of God. Yet just because we are not God, the guidance we need most concerns not the ultimate choice between good and evil but the little choices that can sway the balance between happiness and misery in human lives day by day.[36]

Of course, readers often complain that theories of ethics do not provide guidance for specific everyday moral problems. Often that sort of advice is not what the writers intended. The problem in Barth's ethics, however, is more fundamental. He appears to deny that there is any basis for such guidance. An ethical theory can only provide specific guidance if it includes some general propositions. In order to decide what to do in a particular case, we need to examine our choices for action in the light of either some assessment of what persons generally need and desire (act- or rule-teleology) or some rules that prescribe the general sort of acts that persons ought to perform (rule-deontology). Ethical reflection in an act-deontology, which precludes reference to common goals or to general rules, is extremely difficult.

Barth's insistence on the freedom and initiative of God, however, seems to limit human ethics to act-deontology. On the one hand, no generalizations about God's will can be permitted. That would reduce God to an object and restrict his freedom to act. On the other hand, no moral requirements can be built on anything but the will of God. That would substitute human goals and human reason for the Word of God. Though the *analogia fidei* allows us to trust God's persistent intentions toward the world, it does not allow moral reason to trace them in general terms. Obedience to the requirements of the moment is all that marks a faithful ethics. Moral argument, moral uncertainty, and moral justifications belong to that closed-off realm of human speech untouched by the Word.

For all its theological integrity, Barth's position is impossible for a public ethics. If we are to choose our actions by reason and defend them publicly by argument, we must either limit the freedom of God or abandon the metaethics that bases all moral meanings on God's will. Once the ethical implications of Barth's work began to come clear, many theologians were prepared to do one or the other. Their choice to preserve the integrity of ethics at the price of the rigor Barth had introduced into theology led to conflicts among the men who had begun the crisis theology. The sharpest dispute of all, as it turned out, was between Barth and the theologian who had been his associate in the early days of the movement, Emil Brunner.

NOTES

1. Karl Barth, *The Epistle to the Romans,* trans. Edwyn Hoskyns (London: Oxford University Press, 1933), 64.

2. The movement begun by Barth and his associates is also sometimes called neoorthodoxy, but Barth and Brunner both rejected that label as misleading.

"Orthodoxy," Brunner explained, is a term for the doctrinal rigidities that developed after the first generation of reformers. Barth, Brunner, and their associates wanted to be faithful to the founders of Protestantism, but that meant precisely refusing to let the reformers' words define the Word of God. A Protestant orthodoxy was the last thing the dialectical theologians wanted to revive.

3. Rom. 2:15.

4. Karl Barth, *The Word of God and the Word of Man,* trans. Douglas Horton (New York: Harper & Brothers, 1957), 9.

5. It is interesting that, when "situation ethics" tries to demonstrate the uselessness of moral rules, it often draws its examples from wartime. See Joseph Fletcher, *Situation Ethics* (Philadelphia: Westminster Press, 1966).

6. Barth, *The Word of God,* 170–71.

7. Eberhard Busch, *Karl Barth* (Philadelphia: Fortress Press, 1976), 144–45.

8. Barth, *Epistle,* 517.

9. Reinhold Niebuhr, "We Are Men and Not God," *Christian Century,* 27 October 1948, 1139.

10. Karl Barth, *Protestant Theology in the Nineteenth Century* (Valley Forge, Pa.: Judson Press, 1973), 266–312.

11. Immanuel Kant, *Groundwork of the Metaphysics of Morals,* trans. H. J. Paton (New York: Harper & Row, 1964), 61.

12. One important problem that Kant does not consider arises when two apparently valid imperatives come into conflict. If keeping a promise to my friend would mean ignoring the needs of an aged parent who suddenly wants my attention, which of these apparent duties should I fulfill? We cannot deal with this problem in Kantian ethics here beyond taking note of it. Some of Kant's critics think that, in fact, it cannot be solved. See W. D. Ross, *Kant's Ethical Theory* (Oxford: At the Clarendon Press, 1954).

13. See Robert E. Willis, *The Ethics of Karl Barth* (Leiden: E. J. Brill, 1971), 157, 171.

14. This helps to explain why Barth's ethic of the Word of God is nothing like "situation ethics," even though both systems are critical of general moral rules. Situation ethics identifies love as the appropriate goal for all human action and asks, in teleological fashion, what actions one should choose to produce the most loving results. Both this act teleology and Barth's act-deontology agree that there are no general rules that can tell us what we ought to do, but Barth would insist that no human experience or human desires can guide us either. For an interpretation that takes Barth, Brunner, and Bonhoeffer all as "situationists," see, however, Joseph Fletcher, *Situation Ethics* (Philadelphia: Westminster Press, 1966).

15. We will see later that Bonhoeffer criticized Barth's theology as "revelational positivism." Barth did not like the label and did not accept the objections.

16. Romans 14.

17. Barth, *Epistle,* 515.

18. Barth borrowed this title of a treatise by Anselm of Canterbury (1033–1109) for a work of his own published in Germany in 1930. See Karl Barth, *Anselm: Fides Quarens Intellectum* (London: SCM Press, 1960).

19. Part of these lectures of 1928–1929 have recently been published in an English, comprehensive edition of Barth's works. See Karl Barth, *Ethics* (Grand Rapids: Wm. B. Eerdmans, 1981). *Church Dogmatics* was the work of Barth's life. While Barth planned a major volume on ethics which in fact was never written, it is consistent with his theology that for the most part he treats issues in ethics as they arise in connection with dogmatics. Readers who are especially interested in Barth's ethics should consult *Church Dogmatics,* 2/2 (The Command of God); 3/4 (The Command of God the Creator); and 4/3 ("The Vocation of Man" and "The Holy Spirit and the Sending of the Christian Community"). The unusual form of these references results from the appearance of several "volumes" of the *Dogmatics* as more than one book. Thus 2/2 refers to the second book of "Volume" 2. The complete set is bound as 13 books, but comprises only 4 "volumes."

20. See David Tracy, *The Analogical Imagination* (New York: Crossroad, 1981), 405–15.

21. Rom. 1:19–20.

22. John Calvin, *Institutes of the Christian Religion,* ed. John T. McNeill (Philadelphia: Westminster Press, 1960), 1:277.

23. Barth, *Anselm,* 26–27.

24. Karl Barth, *The Holy Ghost and the Christian Life,* Trans. R. Birch Hoyle (London: Frederick Mueller, 1938).

25. Barth, *The Holy Ghost,* 81.

26. Max Scheler, *Formalism in Ethics and Non-Formal Ethics of Values,* trans. Manfred S. Frings and Roger L. Funk (Evanston, Ill.: Northwestern University Press, 1973).

27. See William K. Frankena, *Ethics,* 2d ed. (Englewood Cliffs, N.J.: Prentice-Hall, 1973), 95–96.

28. Barth, *Ethics,* 215.

29. Barth, *The Word of God,* 279.

30. Barth, *The Holy Ghost,* 14.

31. Barth is primarily concerned at this point to prevent his readers from understanding his work as a version of traditional "natural law" theory, but his criticism would apply equally well to those who hope to find a secure basis for ethics in scientific discoveries. Barth would probably conclude that sociobiology, for example, relies too much on general conclusions about human and animal behavior and fails to provide specific guidance for persons faced with moral dilemmas.

32. Barth, *The Holy Ghost,* 21.

33. Ibid., 72.

34. Ibid., 81, 82.

35. Ibid., 59.

36. Niebuhr, "We Are Men," 1139.

3
EMIL BRUNNER:
CRITICAL COOPERATION

Karl Barth's theology confronts human moral perplexity with the awesome freedom of God. In place of our faulty and inexact attempts to formulate moral requirements in laws and rules, Barth offers the certainty of obedience to the Word. Yet, as we have seen, it becomes almost impossible to *speak* of this obedience, to formulate its directives in a way that explains our actions to others and provides some guidance for their own choices.

It becomes almost impossible to do ethics in public terms. Christians can invite others to join them in obedience, but they cannot explain in advance what obedience will require or why. Yet the important acts of obedience almost invariably have a public significance. This is true, certainly, of decisions about law and government that Christians must make in cooperation with those of other faiths and of no explicit faith who share the same society. In our places of work or in voluntary organizations, it is also true of decisions that require the cooperation of many persons before they can become effective. It is even true for many personal decisions about where we work and how we will live— decisions for which we not only want the freedom to choose, we also want others to understand and accept our choices. In these ways, a great deal of the Christian life is also a public life, and our acts of obedience are also public decisions. For these we seek the understanding and cooperation of others, and if we expect to receive it, we must find ways to explain our choices.

Barth expresses a sovereign disdain for all such explanations, and there is an important point to his objections. Christians who set out to explain the requirements of obedience are all too likely to end up trimming the Word to suit the sensitivities of the audience. We must, Barth insists, proclaim the Word without apology if we expect to win others to obedience.

Nevertheless, the most common public response to bold proclamation is not conversion. It is indifference. When we declare the undistorted command without regard for the preferences of the hearers, we are more likely to speak without hypocrisy, but we are less likely to be heard. Dietrich Bonhoeffer, writing from a prison cell in 1944, began to understand this problem in the theology of crisis:

> Barth was the first theologian to begin the criticism of religion, and that remains his really great merit; but he put in its place a positivist doctrine of revelation which says, in effect, like it or lump it. . . . In the place of religion there now stands the church—that is in itself biblical—but the world is in some degree made to depend on itself and left to its own devices, and that's the mistake.[1]

Bonhoeffer was concerned about how faithful Christians could participate responsibly in shaping their societies. Barth's mistake was, not so much that he left the world to wander without direction, but that it is left to *its own* direction. Barth failed to provide a way to relate the concrete command of God to the everyday business of political decisions and public discussion. The Christian's "like it or lump it" does not leave society unable to make these decisions, but it means that there will be no practical way to relate those choices to the Christian's understanding of what God requires. By 1944 Bonhoeffer had reason enough to fear a society formed without responsible Christian participation.

Of course, there are many ideas around which a society can organize its public choices, not all of them as reprehensible as the Nazi idolatry of race and nation. Utilitarian philosophers in England advocated the democratic principle that decisions should be made to secure the greatest happiness of the greatest number of persons. In Germany Kant had argued for a social system that would leave persons free to follow their own moral reason, for only a life based on reason makes one worthy of happiness. Others, in a less optimistic frame of mind, understood public power as a necessary check on the willfulness and self-concern of individuals. Any of these theories provides a systematic basis for making public decisions, and every society, bureaucracy, or legislature chooses some such principle for decision. The refusal of Christians to participate in that choice would hardly be noticed.

Indeed, there have always been Christians who find the separation of faith from public choice appropriate and desirable. Apart from the perennially popular opinion that religion is a good thing but "business is business," there is a tendency in Protestant social thought toward an acknowledgment that life in society must be governed by tougher, less trusting rules than the standards which should prevail in a community of Christians. This expresses itself both in the sectarian impulse to form small communities of faith where the Christian standards can prevail and in the Lutheran way of thinking about "two kingdoms," which allows the Christian who happens to be a ruler or a magistrate to conduct that public office by a different standard than applies in private Christian life. If Barth's "theological positivism" simply permits the world to go on its own way, many Christians, past and present, would have no problem with it. They follow Christ's way when they can and the world's way when they must, and they acknowledge the difference between the two as a basic reality in human life.

However, none of the authors we are considering closely can fully accept that position. For Brunner and Bonhoeffer, no less than for Karl Barth himself, the meaning of moral terms is tied to the will of God. What things are good and what acts are right simply cannot be determined without some consideration of God's activity and intentions. Unless public choices are matters of complete moral indifference, they, too, must be related to the divine command. The old dualism of a Christian good determined by the will of God and a secular good defined by standards of efficiency, order, or human happiness will not suffice in the confusions of this new age.

The metaethical position that all moral terms derive their meaning from the will of God conflicts, however, with the theological position that God's will must be free and unbound by human systems. If a theologian rejects the dualistic attempt to distinguish divine and human meanings of 'good' he or she must face at once the dilemma posed at the end of chapter 2: either the meaning of 'good' must be separated from the will of God altogether, or the freedom of God must be interpreted in a way that fits it to the needs of human choice and action.

Bonhoeffer and Brunner chose the latter course. They chose it reluctantly because they were fearful of a return to the uncritical cultural theology of the era before the war, but they did choose it because the alternative—finding a purely human meaning for 'good' and leaving the world to "depend on its own devices"—was clearly impossible. It would mean shutting the Christians off from any effective impact on the lives of those around them. It would accept the alienation of postwar society from the church as an accomplished fact and reduce the social role of the faith to a quaint ritual reminder of a bygone era. Small wonder Brunner argues that "he who thinks as a missionary" understands immediately the need for this risky enterprise of rendering the will of God intelligible in human terms.[2]

If God's will is to be understood, God's freedom must be expressed in order. A God who is completely free at any moment to do and to demand anything whatsoever is as incomprehensible to me as a completely free person would be. Mere freedom is nothing I can count on. If the only thing I know for certain about you is that you are free, I will have to plan my life around some other, more definitive, set of expectations. That, Brunner and Bonhoeffer began to see, is precisely where crisis theology leaves society with respect to God. In destroying the old unions of faith and culture, "throne and altar," God and European civilization, Barth had provided no reliable expectations in their place. The Christian who may be "a realist or an idealist . . . a Pietist, perhaps, but quite as well a Communist"[3] will have nothing to say to the world's choices.

Barth, of course, agreed that the will of God must be quite specific in each situation, but his insistence that the *analogia fidei* begins always with God and never with humanity was intended to prevent a generalization from one specific situation to the next. It was just that step that Bonhoeffer and Brunner decided finally to permit.

Crisis theology was correct to insist that God is not bound to act according to patterns simply because these seem right to humanity, but this stipulation does not mean that God acts without any intelligible pattern at all. Bonhoeffer and Brunner suggested that both the historical experience of the church and the natural regularities of the "orders of creation" are places where the consistency of God's will can be encountered, places where the will of God becomes available as a guide for human action. To be sure, God's choice of the church is often a scandal to human observers, who would prefer to find the divine presence in more refined company. The requirements of the orders of creation often chafe those who seek less restrained expressions of sexuality, or authority, or acquisitiveness. Nevertheless, we must not turn the human tendency to corrupt or distort God's choices into a reason to insist that God cannot make them.

God's freedom and initiative are the starting point for all moral goodness and all right action. This Bonhoeffer and Brunner continued to affirm, but they also insisted that God's will is systematically expressed in the life of the church and in the orders of creation. In the end we will see that Bonhoeffer stresses the role of the church and the relevance of history. By 1944 Bonhoeffer had come to distrust a straightforward reading of the orders of creation. That, however, is a story for a later chapter. Initially, we must understand the attempt of theology to relate God's will to public choices through a new emphasis on the natural regularities of the family, work, worship, and the state. We must understand Emil Brunner's doctrine of the orders of creation.

The Orders of Creation

Brunner's first major work in theological ethics was published in Zurich in 1932. The primary importance of the will of God is suggested at once in the English title *The Divine Imperative*.[4] Brunner approved this title for the translation, but the original German title conveys better the essential connection he seeks: *Das Gebot und die Ordnungen* (The Commandment and the Orders). Brunner's point is that for human beings there is an inseparable link between the commandment of God and the concrete historical circumstances and natural limitations in which we are set. We encounter the commandment not only in the "general laws of creation, of the preservation and furtherance of life, and of specifically human life" but also in "those existing facts of human corporate life which lie at the root of all historical life as unalterable presuppositions, which, although their historical forms may vary, are unalterable in their fundamental structure and, at the same time, relate and unite men to one another in a definite way."[5]

What do these orders include? Obviously, there is no simple list that names exactly those relationships that are orders of creation. Brunner has in mind a whole set of interdependent institutions that set the context for human life. Marriage and family are included, of course, but so are economic orders of work and wealth. The institutions of government are orders of creation, and so are the institutions of education, art, and science. Obviously natural bonds—for example parent-child relationships—are included, but so are roles like citizenship, work, and ownership, which seem to depend more on historical and social development. To speak of the orders of creation then is not a way to sharply distinguish natural relationships from those that are merely conventional. The orders in which we may encounter the commandment of God encompass virtually all of the institutions in which human life is lived.

The imperatives that we meet in the orders do not always strike us with the force of "Thus saith the Lord." The orders impose on us, first, the material requirements that govern making, building, or cultivating, and then, too, the social requirements that govern cooperative human action. Those who act within the orders of creation must observe the strength limits of construction materials, for instance. They must know the physics that governs their use of tools, but they must also follow the demands of trust and justice that make it possible for them to work with others. In the problems of discerning the material and social require- ments of human life, Christians have neither special insight nor spe- cial obligations that distinguish them from the rest of humanity. "[A] Christian engineer does not build 'Christian bridges' but solid bridges."[6]

In this way, Brunner seeks to recapture the typically Protestant idea of vocation or calling and put it to use in a new way. It is true, as Luther insisted, that any occupation can be a Christian vocation. The re- former's objections to medieval clericalism are sound, but they are sound because not only our work but everything we do within the orders of creation must be seen as a response to God's call. Our vocation is nothing less than our life itself, limited as it is by natural and historical circumstances, shaped as it has been by our choices and by the choices of others. "Only through the perception of this truth is the ascetic conception of life completely eliminated; at the same time this truth eliminates all mere 'secularism' of outlook. One who, in faith, dwells within these orders, and renders service through them while he is working in *the world,* is also working in the *Kingdom of God*."[7]

One can hardly imagine a more striking contrast to Barth's insistence that human activity can never be even a first step toward the kingdom of heaven.[8] In place of a doctrine of the Word of God that cuts across all our ways of understanding ourselves, Brunner has put a doctrine of vocation that makes our responsiveness to the human situation a form of obedience to the divine command.

Brunner understood, however, that such a Christian vocation could be mistaken for a rather comfortable way of life. The idea that Chris- tian life is lived in responsiveness to the orders could lead the faithful to see it as their task to do just what the world wants, fulfilling expectations so skillfully that they simply disappear into their surroundings or following the material and social imperatives so diligently that they achieve a thoroughly conventional success.

Brunner tries to avoid this by emphasizing that mere observance of the orders does not grasp their real relation to God.

Adaptation to the existing order, therefore, because it has been created by God, is the *first* point in the Christian ethic; but it is never the last point.

The first thing is always what God wills as Creator; but—even apart from our sin—it is not the last. For He wills to lead the creation out beyond itself, into the perfecting of all things. God does not preserve the world simply in order to preserve it, but in order that he may perfect it.[9]

In view of this, the appropriate Christian response to the orders of creation is not mere adaptation. It is *critical cooperation.*[10] Nothing will be gained by trying to circumvent the orders, following some utopian scheme that promises to do away with the constraints of family or hoping for a time when people will live in peace without a state, but Christians need not take the family and the state just as they find them. Christian vocation within the orders is work within the kingdom of God because, like God's own work, it aims at the perfection of the orders.

The principal guideline for this work is love. Love is an immediate responsiveness to the needs of the neighbor, and precisely because of this immediacy, it can never be reduced to a rule. Love has that power to escape formulations and shatter expectations that Barth found in the Word of God. For Brunner, however, love is never the sole guide to action. A wise love stays well within the limits that the orders of creation describe, but when those boundaries are hard to discern, the immediacy of loving concern for the neighbor can be decisive for action. For example, Brunner finds that economic life, as an order of creation, encompasses both a command to work and a permission to enjoy the good things that work creates.[11] Both asceticism and a heedless consumption of the products of other people's labor are thus prohibited in a right ordering of economic life, but the range of possibilities between the two prohibitions is still exceedingly wide. It is the function of love in modern capitalism, no less than in the simpler world of Jesus' parables, to fix our attention on the needs of others and to help us choose alternatives that serve something more than our own needs and desires.

> Ultimately, therefore, even within this system of Capitalism the same simple rules of Christian conduct hold good as in any of the earlier more patriarchal economic conditions; i.e., to renounce worry, to refuse to be enslaved in spirit, not to seek our own, but that which profits our neighbour, not to assert our own rights at the expense of others, not to be covetous, or acquisitive, or greedy, not to become inhuman for the sake of things, to be ready to sacrifice our own possessions for the needs of others.[12]

Economic life must be conducted under the command to work and the permission to enjoy and within the forms of work made available in our own time in history. What is open to the Christian is simply to live within the constraints of the economic order and to choose among its options with a sincere concern for the neighbor's need. Love cannot replace the rules and regulations of economic life, but it can prevent us from exploiting those rules in ways that only serve our narrow self-interest. "As long as we human beings live in this world, where there are systems, justice is as indispensable as love," Brunner declared in his later work *Justice and the Social Order.* "The man of love, as soon as he has to act in the world of institutions, turns his love into justice. He knows that if he did otherwise, he would ruin, destroy the world of institutions."[13]

The world of institutions is the historically given form of the orders of creation in which we are called to live our lives before God. Thus does Brunner unite the divine imperative and the demand for public decisions in political, economic, and personal life. Formally, the stark metaethics of crisis theology are retained: "The Good is simply and solely the will of God."[14] Limited human purposes and human desires do not enter into the meaning of moral terms, but the normative requirements of the orders of creation must be framed by human intelligence in critical cooperation with the existing institutional structures. To say that a choice serves human happiness or supports some system that people happen to desire is never by itself a moral justification of the decision, for that is not what moral terms mean. "The Good is simply and solely the will of God." Nevertheless, no claim to know the good or to do the right can be upheld without reference to the things that sustain human life in the basic orders of family, work, religion, state, and culture which God has willed. Thus every moral claim is subject to review, not only by those who profess obedience to the will of God, but also by all who know the practical limitations of life in society's present institutions.

The idea of an order of creation is still very general, and Brunner's conviction that, say, the central realities of marriage or the state must remain constant throughout history and in all societies forces him to very abstract statements in his presentation of the orders: Marriage is a "school" for community in which we learn that we cannot live as solitary individuals.[15] The state is the realization of community in its most inclusive form.[16] Nevertheless, as these ideas are elaborated and carefully related to existing social realities, Brunner provides some very specific guidelines for public decisions. He has much to say about each of the orders of creation separately, but there are a few main themes that appear to set the direction for his specific normative conclusions.

The Primacy of Preservation

Brunner's discussion of the orders of creation stresses the primacy of *preservation*, the importance of preserving order where it exists. To be sure, the principle of critical cooperation stops us short of smug satisfaction with the way things are, but Brunner shares with many of his Protestant contemporaries an appreciation of the difficulties that beset every attempt to create social order, however imperfect. Because all persons who have power tend to exploit their communities for personal gain, while self-centered concerns of the people lead them to evade responsibility where possible, every political community is constantly threatened with dissolution, and in the end all states fall back on force to maintain the minimal requirements of order. The resulting forms of government are far from ideal and always rest on more or less obvious injustices, but a realistic appraisal of human sinfulness leads Christians to a sober respect for the achievements embodied in any government at all. Because no change in political arrangements can eliminate sin, which is the root cause of disorder, Christians are reluctant to exchange any system that works tolerably well for the mere idea of an order which—as an idea—might work much better.

This traditional respect for existing orders and authorities posed a special problem for theologians of Brunner's generation. The widespread feeling that the new world situation made all existing forms of government obsolete touched even the relative stability of Swiss politics. Barth's insistence on the freedom of the Word of God offered one ready solution to the problem: The Word that cuts across all institutions and shatters our moral expectations may demand that we sweep away the old political order completely and replace it with some new form that better suits God's concrete commandment. Barth did not himself endorse revolution, but his theology could not in principle exclude it.

Brunner's reliance on the orders of creation as the place where God's Word is heard placed him in a more difficult position. He did not want to ignore the cries for revolutionary renewal of the political order, but he understood that if the state as an order of creation represents the divine commandment, "only unavoidable necessity will avail to protect this dangerous action [i.e., revolution] from the reproach of rebellion against God."[17]

Put more exactly, the problem is that a revolution seems to attempt to create order by destroying it. This paradox never is easily untangled, but when the existing political system has been identified as the gift of God's creation and life within its historical limitations has been called our vocation, almost nothing can be said that makes sense of the effort to overthrow it. "In itself it is impossible to justify revolution from the ethical point of view even when it takes place for the sake of a better order, for it elevates anarchy to the level of principle, and in so doing it destroys the basis of all morality."[18] Revolution seems to be the one act of Christian obedience that could not be a public decision, for it defies the acceptance of history on which the ethic of the orders of creation is based.

In the years that followed the publication of *The Divine Imperative*, Brunner's reluctance to endorse revolutionary change was stretched to the breaking point by the collapse of Germany's fragile experiment in democracy and the rise of Nazi totalitarianism. We will see in chapter 4 that he came to accept an argument for a right to revolution based on natural law, an appeal *in extremis* that would permit citizens to overthrow the order of the state to prevent the complete ruin of all the orders. The primacy of preservation does not oblige us to accept evil just because it exists, but it forbids us to risk the good that does exist for the sake of a possible improvement. A social ethic formed on Brunner's principles may be quite critical of certain features of social and economic life (Brunner himself never quite reconciled his early socialist convictions with the realities of European capitalism), but on the whole it will be a conservative ethic. Appreciation for the achievements of the prevailing order induces one not to take risks and makes it difficult to understand those who see so little hope for their own future that they would risk everything on the chance for a total social change.

So it is not surprising that talk of revolution comes easier to some theologians today than it did to Brunner. The theology of liberation, formulated in Latin America three decades after Brunner's major work in ethics, begins by identifying with the poorest of the poor and sees quite differently the risks and costs that go with maintaining a social order that accepts such poverty as a fact of life.[19] Against that backdrop, we see clearly that Brunner's vision is European and that his questions are posed in terms of people who have much to lose in any failure of the social system.

A theology which confronts the reality of massive human suffering is rightly suspicious of any ethics that advises us to preserve the existing order simply because it exists. Nevertheless, a theological identification with poverty and oppression taken by itself is not a sufficient guide to action. It may give people the will and the sense of self that enable them to change the system, but it may also call down forces of repression and inhibit incremental changes that can be made within the material and social constraints of the present structure of the orders. What will happen when the spirit of liberation is loosed cannot be predicted on theological grounds alone. It requires some knowledge of the structures of society and a careful assessment of one's political allies, who may see the need for liberating actions even if they do not share the theology of liberation. Which courses of action will prove truly liberating cannot be decided by a theology that demands justice. It requires a detailed knowledge of the economic and social forces that are at work to maintain the obvious targets of revolutionary ire and a comprehensive theory of the world's political economy to guide the new order toward a satisfactory meeting of the needs that first impelled theological concern.[20]

Brunner's first theological formulations reflect the need of the powerful to preserve the order that exists, rather than the desperation of the powerless. As we will see, he eventually had to recognize that there can be justifiable demands for revolution. What his account of the orders of creation offers for a contemporary global ethics is not the insistence on preservation but the recognition that even radical change must be a form of critical cooperation with the material imperatives that limit what we can do and with the social imperatives that require us to do it in concert with others. Brunner's career provided few opportunities to rethink his ethics in a social context like that which gives rise to liberation theology. We will see a much closer approach to revolutionary change in Bonhoeffer's "venture of responsibility" in chapter 6. At just that point, however, the respect for social facts that Brunner requires becomes crucial for Bonhoeffer, too. These systematic considerations give Brunner's social ethics a relevance to radical change that goes far beyond the rather conservative substance of his own politics.

Interdependence

A second emphasis in Brunner's doctrine of the orders is on *interdependence*. Here marriage is the important illustration, as the problem of the state illustrated the importance of preservation. What is said about marriage also characterizes human relationships generally, in citizenship, labor, and culture as well as in the family. Marriage teaches us that the pattern of all true relationships is complementary. The lasting bonds of life develop when each party provides a strength that the other lacks.

Brunner's Christian vision of human relationships may be contrasted with the classical ideal found in Aristotle. For Aristotle the model for all relationships is friendship rather than marriage. Friendship in its true form exists only between persons who are alike.[21] Where there are differences—as between husbands and wives, young and old, rulers and subjects—there may still be friendship, but it is always difficult, and we call those relationships friendship only by analogy to the situation in which friends enjoy each other's company precisely because they do not need anything from each other.

The Christian ideal, by contrast, stresses differences. Marriage is built, not only on the sexual differences between husband and wife, but on their complementarity of affective styles and personal strengths. If Brunner's stress on masculine initiative and feminine nurturance seems old-fashioned to us,[22] we must look beyond those stereotypes to the underlying conviction that it is the differences between persons which make intimacy possible.

Not only the intimacy of marriage, but the satisfactions of all relationships depend on difference. Marriage as an order of creation teaches us that, despite the damage to our pride, we must admit our own needs and insufficiency, and we must reject every philosophy or social scheme which denies those realities.

Interdependence calls into question the values of individualism. While we take a natural pride in asserting ourselves and standing out from the community, Brunner sees that this self-assertion is, paradoxically, a force for uniformity. To be an individual, I have to be self-sufficient. I try to make myself independent by denying the needs and weaknesses that bind me to others' strengths. Hence, behind a superficial diversity of taste in dress and mannerisms, modern individualists are more like one another than people ever were before. Genuine uniqueness binds me to others. I can be an individual only if I already have everything that they might give me, only if I already am everything that they are.

Again, it is in marriage that we learn this nettlesome lesson best. While Brunner acknowledges that marriage and family relationships do change in history, he insists that there are "immutable constants" not to be ignored.

> Men have never borne and never will bear children. In spite of all intellectual development, men and their specific function have remained clearly and characteristically distinguishable as a species from women. A certain

type of female emancipation, now fortunately on the wane, which put forward a claim to equality with men, is one of the forms of the rationalistic individualism of modern times.[23]

Brunner is not simply indulging in male supremacism here. He is equally critical of the view that takes the male role as an excuse for arbitrary domination and lordship, and he writes elsewhere with genuine sympathy for the growing demand of women for a place in life outside the home.[24] Nevertheless, in contrast to those who would criticize every aspect of family life as a vestige of the patriarchal, oppressive societies of the past, Brunner clearly believes that there is a central reality embodied in the traditional role differentiations that cannot be faulted and must not be changed. "What is for the man in the street simply a fact of nature with a very vague claim to legality is in the Christian faith an order of creation, a natural difference ordained by God as a criterion."[25]

No theologian today can simply accept Brunner's legitimation of male and female social roles. The particular features of human interdependence that he identifies arouse our suspicions no less than his calm assurance that the order we have is always better than no order at all. The problem with his ordering of male-female relations is more fundamental, however, for it rests on a claim about "immutable constants" in human society that is crucial to his whole system.

The difficulty, of course, is to discern precisely where the immutable differences ordained by God end and historical contingency begins. Confronted by the same problem, feminist writers remind us that sex-role distinctions that are so pervasive as to seem universal, especially in Western societies, may nonetheless be the product of historic choices, rather than natural requirements.[26] To say that something has always been does not prove that it cannot be otherwise, and it is the latter, stronger claim that Brunner's "immutable constants" must make. Even among Brunner's contemporaries, Reinhold Niebuhr concluded that there are no "natural" human institutions, no single thing that comes to us unchanged by human choice and history.[27] No constant center can be isolated, and so there is no element that we can surely identify as God's will, rather than our own.

Brunner will not go so far. Indeed, he finds the constancies fairly easy to identify. The problem is that they include certain fundamental differentiations and certain imbalances of power that a modern mind would rather not acknowledge. Among the constants that become normative criteria for Christians are masculine and feminine roles in marriage and the family, differentiations of wealth and function in economic life, and hierarchies of power and authority in the state. To be sure, these distinctions can be exploited by those who would use them for their own benefit. Brunner acknowledges that in the form we have them these divinely ordered differentiations may be severely distorted, but he insists that the inequalities that arise from such distinctions cannot in themselves be unjust. They are part of the orders of creation.

This leads to a second consequence of interdependence. Just as Brunner rejects the modern individualism that will, he thinks, make us all come out very much the same, so he rejects strict equality as a goal for society. Insofar as human beings are different, they are unequal. An ethic based on the divine command encountered in the orders of creation will respect those differences and will not attempt to eradicate the inequalities they imply.

On this point, Brunner maintains a position quite different from most of his contemporaries, Catholic and Protestant. After World War I, the conviction grew in some quarters that all inequalities between persons are artificial distinctions that reflect the interests of those who have wealth and power, rather than real differences that ought to be respected.

Theologians generally have made more moderate criticism of inequality, but they, too, have treated it as morally suspect. Inequality, they have suggested, is a functional necessity. We permit differences of wealth, privilege, and power only because they are necessary to secure certain things that make life better for everyone.[28] To have skilled services in medicine or technology, we must reward those who undertake the long and difficult training in those skills. To have efficient production in industry and stable order in government, capable persons must be encouraged to accept the burdens of leadership and must also be provided authority to lead once they are chosen. Nevertheless, what requires watching is not the provision of incentives and rewards but the invariable tendency of those who have skills and authority to claim rather more than their position strictly requires. Inequalities always tend to grow beyond functional necessity, so that the question of ethics is always the critical question, Can the pattern of inequality that exists be justified?

Brunner's position is somewhat different. Because he treats the functional requirements of society as part of the order of creation and not as mere human conveniences, he tends to ask whether the existing pattern of inequality is functioning well, not whether it can be justified.

Human interdependence is manifest when persons who have different functions serve one another freely in the different places they occupy in the social hierarchy.

The idea that a person's vocation is bound not only to a task, but to a place that task occupies in the social order, is deeply rooted in Brunner's thought and in the Calvinist tradition on which he relies.[29] Disruptions occur when some persons withhold their best service for personal gain. Calvinist thought links this emphasis on interdependence to a now outmoded economic theory that makes the circulation of wealth, rather than productivity, the principal determinant of general prosperity. Thus it is not the social hierarchy itself that creates the gross economic inequalities we observe. Hierarchy, in fact, promotes the mutual dependence of one vocation on another and so contributes to the levelling of purely economic differences. So a modern interpreter of Calvin writes:

> In a society ordered according to the purpose of God, there is, therefore a mutual communication of goods. This communication does not completely eliminate, but rather it attenuates, economic inequalities. If nothing fettered and clogged this free circulation of wealth, society would, through a continuous movement of reciprocity flowing from human solidarity, tend toward a relative economic equality. This equality would be differentiated according to the real vocation of each person.[30]

Brunner's ethic of critical cooperation reflects this Calvinist understanding of social inequality. The critical question is not directed to the differentiation and the pattern of inequality as such but to the way that individuals live out their vocations in that pattern. Brunner's dissatisfaction with the magnitude of prevailing inequalities is sincere, but his questions about it are not as fundamental as those of Reinhold Niebuhr, to say nothing of the more radical socialists or contemporary liberation theology.

In economic life, no less than in the life of the family, Brunner remains convinced that some structures persist which are truly part of the created order, which express the will of God rather than any human expectations. Niebuhr's insistence that every relationship in which human beings participate bears the mark of human creativity and of human sin as well finds no echo in Brunner's thought at this point. Niebuhr attempts to evaluate every instance of inequality, to distinguish the elements of functional necessity in it from the elements of self-seeking. Brunner does not want to encourage wealth and luxury, but he finds the efforts to strictly define the inequalities required by vocation an exercise in "false Puritanical legalism, which ought to be most definitely rejected, not only on general cultural grounds, but also on grounds of faith."[31] Critical cooperation suggests a society in which economic inequalities would be far less extreme than they are today, but critical cooperation requires rather less suspicion of the sources of inequality than Niebuhr had. For some today, Brunner's account may provide sufficient guidance. Most ethicists, however, will seek to appropriate Brunner's insights on human interdependence without his acceptance of social inequality, just as they will acknowledge the constraints of social reality without his inclination to preserve the reality as it exists. On these points, liberation theology and feminist theology have taught us more critical habits of thought.

No General Rules

A third characteristic of Brunner's ethics is his rejection of general moral rules. This, too, derives from his insistence on the uniqueness of persons and their vocations within the orders of creation, and so Brunner's criticism of rule-ethics develops quite differently from Barth's.[32] Barth argues that general moral rules limit the freedom of God. Rules attempt to reduce the encounter with God's free word to a predictable event, and so they must be rejected on theological grounds. Brunner, by contrast, complains that general moral rules are inadequate to human experience. The variety of ethical theories— deontologies, teleologies, and the rest—testifies to the inability of any rational system to make complete sense of the moral life in terms that apply alike to all persons.

> Each ethical system approaches the phenomenon of morality in very different ways; each is right, up to a point, compared with the rest; the excellence of one shows up the weakness in another; thus, in varying degrees, each has its own particular value and each has its special weakness; thus this unsatisfactory situation cannot be overcome by any kind of "synthetic ethics."[33]

The problem here is the weakness of human reason—and we will have much more to say about it in the next chapter—which leads to a peculiar inaccuracy in every attempt to speak generally about morality. Since Aristotle, justice has been understood as *suum cuique* (to each his own). "Justice makes no free gift; it gives precisely what is due to the other, no more and no less."[34] To achieve this evenhandedness, however, systems of justice must deal with persons as if they were the same, as if all were subject to a single, common rule. Such justice is obviously superior to the tyranny of the strong over the weak, where the rule is "To each as much as he can take." Still, that does not eliminate the real differences between persons that renders all attempts to treat people according to general formulae artificial and unsatisfactory. The uneasy sense that systems of justice based on rules and reasons reduce persons to general things that can be treated in general ways links up with the Christian's theological claim that the orders of creation in their diversity and particularity express the will of God and provide the place where God's commandment is encountered. The theologian acknowledges the accuracy of the common human complaint that all systems of ethics are inadequate, then points to the source of the difficulty: systems of ethics cannot encounter persons in the created order in their diversity and in the specificity of their vocations, while human life itself is made up of those encounters. This does not mean that Christians can ignore justice or systematic ethics; but they must avoid the common mistake of ending their moral efforts there; and they must reject the claim that, with a little more care in the theory or a little further refinement of the rules, a systematic ethic that would comprehend the diversity of human moral experience could be devised.

Brunner and Ethical Theory

Brunner's insistence on preserving such order as exists, his stress on interdependence, and his rejection of general moral rules together generate a normative system of considerable richness. The problem is to determine what sort of normative system it is. The suspicion of moral generalizations and the insistence on the specificity of each person and vocation suggest an act-ethic not unlike Barth's. Yet Brunner clearly does not share Barth's conviction that all human moral enterprises are merely vain attempts to limit the freedom of God. The things that persons intend to do in their work, their governments, their families, and their churches are not insignificant. They are, indeed, a part of the Kingdom of God.

In terms of ethical theory, Brunner can perhaps best be described as an *act-teleologist*. No set of general moral rules can accurately prescribe what we should do, but the generality that is essential for a public discussion of ethics is provided in the *telos*, the goal toward which moral actions are directed. In Brunner's case, this goal is no single, simple criterion such as human happiness (proposed by the early utilitarians) nor even the maximization of *agape* (suggested by recent "situation ethics"). The *telos* or goal is rather to sustain the whole complex structure of the orders of creation as discerned in scripture and in common human experience. To reach the goal we sometimes need the guidance of rules and systems of justice, especially in matters of government where problems are complex and decisions affect large numbers of people. We do best, however, when we work at our vocations and treat those we encounter with a love that sees in them their unique combination of needs and strengths and joins their lives with ours in interdependence.

Brunner's closest philosophical counterparts would seem to be the English "ideal utilitarians,"[35] who transformed the early utilitarian emphasis on producing the greatest good for the masses of people by insisting that individuals achieve satisfaction only by pursuing a uniquely personal goal that makes a distinctive contribution to human history. There is no evidence that Brunner ever studied these authors closely, and he would doubtless have found their donnish styles and late-Victorian values too stuffy for a world whose moral reflections were propelled by the crisis of a world war. Nevertheless, he shares their concern for a world in which the diversity of human life will not be swallowed up in system and in which the business of ethics will not be obligations that fall on humanity in general but duties and opportunities for service that come to each of us in our particularity.

In any case, Brunner's careful examination of the orders of creation provides a way of thinking about moral decisions that is far more open to public discussion than Barth's ethics of the Word, without losing the specificity of the moral demand on each individual.

The Barth-Brunner Debate

When Brunner began his work in ethics, he thought he was simply providing a needed amplification of the points Barth had been making in *The Epistle to the Romans* and the lectures and articles that subsequently established the framework of dialectical theology. It came as something of a shock, therefore, when Barth vigorously repudiated Brunner's whole effort in ethics. Barth not only insisted that Brunner had misunderstood him; he said that if he had written in ways that allowed such a misrepresentation, he must have stated his own position wrongly. In the debate which ensued, Barth made his most emphatic statement that ethics as a human enterprise simply has no basis. Knowledge of the good, which is bound up with knowing the will of God, cannot be achieved by systematic inquiry. Even knowing that we do not know requires an initiative from God.

The disagreement between Barth and Brunner terminated the collaboration that had spread the theology of the Word of God through the pages of *Zwischen den Zeiten*. Growing theological differences among the editors, compounded by disagreements over the rising tide of German nationalism, put an end to the journal in the fall of 1933. In 1934 Brunner summarized his differences with Barth in an essay titled "Nature and Grace," to which Barth responded with a pamphlet eloquently titled "No!"[36]

However, just because the Barth-Brunner debate had such a significant impact on Protestant theology at the time, we must be careful not to overstate the differences between them. Although much depends on the issue, the point of contention is small indeed, and we need to isolate and identify it before we consider its implications.

Barth and Brunner do not disagree on basic conclusions in normative ethics. When asked what Christians ought to do, what social changes seem to be needed, and which values in family and public life are worth preserving, Barth and Brunner would give largely the same answers. Years later they would argue whether the Communism that dominated Eastern Europe after World War II should be condemned as morally evil, but in 1934, whatever differences they might have had over specific issues in ethics would not have sparked the intense debate that occurred. Brunner's act-teleology differs significantly from Barth's act-deontology in theory, but the results of their normative reflections were very similar.

Neither was the Barth-Brunner debate about metaethics, the meaning of moral terms.[37] Barth and Brunner agreed that 'good' and 'right' mean what God wills. Brunner's readiness to accept a consistent divine intention in creation does not imply that the divine command is only incidental in ethics. Rather, the regularities of creation would have no moral meaning at all for Brunner if they did not give us a place to encounter God's intentions.

What divides Barth and Brunner is precisely the question of our human capabilities to discern those divine intentions, the question whether, apart from revelation, we can know anything at all about what God wills. Theologians have traditionally discussed this question as the problem of the *imago dei*, the "image of God," which Genesis says humanity bore at its first creation.[38] Luther and Calvin, who stressed complete human reliance on God's grace for all moral achievements, tended to speak as if this original likeness to God had been so obliterated by sin as to leave no way for men and women to move directly from knowledge of themselves to a knowledge of God. Barth adopted just that line of argument to block the development of an *analogia entis.*

Brunner believed that the human reality and the Reformers' doctrine were both more complicated than Barth understood. Certainly it is true, he admitted, that sin limits our ability to know God directly in our own experience. There is no valid *analogia entis.* Nevertheless, there is clearly something different about humanity, something that marks us off from the rest of God's creation. Failure to recognize this would be as unrealistic in its own way as that optimistic analogical reasoning which moves directly from the human to the divine. Indeed, we accept this distinction precisely when we speak most decisively about sin and its consequences, for as Luther once noted, we do not preach repentance to sheep. We preach to those who have a capacity to hear and to understand their own sinful condition. It is this *Wortmächtigkeit,* this power to understand a word addressed to us, which is the image of God that remains.[39]

Wortmächtigkeit, "word-power," is a conveniently ambiguous German term for what Brunner has in mind. On the one hand, it might be taken to mean a power to receive the Word, a capacity for revelation present in each human being and waiting to be filled. That interpretation, of course, would provoke Barth's objection that God's Word does not fit neatly into some ordered space in our lives. It breaks in upon us from outside. Brunner can then reply, however, that *Wortmächtigkeit* is no "capacity for revelation." It is simply reason. It is the ability of people to use words rationally and to understand the words of others that marks them off from sheep and cats and parrots, too. This word-power is an obvious fact about human beings. Brunner's idea of the *imago dei* only adds the equally obvious recognition that this power is also essential for the unique human relationship to God.

Reason does not give us the content of revelation, but reason enables us to recognize and understand revelation. In this sense, every rational theology is a "natural theology." Human nature, with its distinctive rational powers, provides the "point of contact" between God's initiative and human responsiveness.

Brunner seems to have realized that this point-of-contact argument renders much of *The Epistle to the Romans* unsatisfactory. While it is true that God's Word shatters the smug and self-sufficient moral categories of an earlier era, the revelation seems addressed precisely to the confusions of postwar Europe, divided by social conflict and shaken by economic failure. It is the limitations of our rationality that this new age shows us most clearly, and the Word of God speaks to those intolerable contradictions. In *Man in Revolt* (1937), Brunner elaborates the confusion in modern thought over the origins of evil.[40] On the one hand, we treat it as an inevitable flaw. The fatalist sees our moral failures as so massive that they become a kind of natural condition for our lives. We cannot even imagine the world without the carnage of war or the desperate poverty of millions of workers. Yet that sense of inevitability which makes the problem so grave also alleviates our sense of responsibility. How can we be blamed for evils that simply must be? A moralist, by contrast, insists on accountability for the evils of the time but seems to imply that, since we are responsible, we could simply stop these evils if we tried. The dark side of human nature is denied, and as a result the outrages we commit are trivialized.

No rational resolution of this problem has been found.

> Thus we are confronted by the fact that in the one instance the deep cleavage in the nature of man is recognized, but responsibility for it is disclaimed, while in the other case, the cleavage is denied. Evidently it is not possible for us to visualize at the same time both the fact of the fatal cleavage in human nature and the fact of full responsibility.[41]

What neither fatalist nor moralist systems can comprehend is however provided in the biblical revelation, which explains that human nature is sinful:

> That means human beings who not only sin now and then, occasionally— that is, every time we do not do the good—but whose very being is defined as sin; but this also means human beings who are fully responsible for all the evil they do, and for the evil in their nature as well. Thus the Biblical revelation permits the contradiction in man's being to be seen without weakening it; at the same time, too, it allows the whole responsibility in action to be seen without weakening it.[42]

This revelation is more than a Word that bursts upon our self-contained reflections from the outside. The Word is a solution to a problem we knew we had but could not solve. It is a resolution which we recognize as correct, even though we acknowledge that it is strange and foreign to the competing and contradictory systems of thought by which we have been trying to understand our existence.

Brunner's work as it developed thus stressed increasingly the contradictions and inadequacies of contemporary philosophy. We cannot explain our human condition to ourselves completely, so we continue with titanic efforts to fashion a system that will encompass reality, or in the twentieth century, we more frequently lapse into an existentialist attitude that embraces the contradiction in reason and tries to escape the dilemma by a sheer act of will. Man is in "revolt" because he rejects the biblical truth about himself and chooses to live in simplistic moralism or willful ambiguity. So all philosophy is inadequate, but it is far from useless. Philosophy poses questions that only revelation can answer comprehensively. *Wortmächtigkeit,* as much by what it cannot do as by what it can, prepares the way for God.

The vigor of Barth's response to Brunner tends to exaggerate the differences between the two men. Both attempted to keep faith with the great reformers, Luther and Calvin, by stressing the pervasive impact of sin on human life and powers. Brunner, despite Barth's accusations, never expressly employs an *analogia entis.* He never uses reason to arrive directly at knowledge about God. What reason teaches us about reality in the last analysis tells us more about the limitations of reason than about God. The point at issue between these two Swiss Protestants is a small one, almost unnoticeable against the whole historic backdrop of Christian controversies, but very important for an age that seeks a theological reorientation after its familiar landmarks and guideposts have all been destroyed.

Barth insists that, when faith seeks a new path, it must be very careful not to map its own human directions on the wilderness. Brunner's emphasis on a distinctive human power of reason, his stress on a capacity which sets us apart from creation is dangerous, not because the distinction is false, but because it focuses our attention in the wrong place. Paul Lehmann aptly summarized the point at issue in an early article on the debate:

> According to Karl Barth, when a man gets too interested in the fact that he is not a cat, he is certain to loose his interest in Christ. According to Brunner, a man must give full weight to the fact that he is not a cat, just because of his interest in Christ.[43]

The danger here is not merely a theologian's quibble. Barth notes that the pro-Nazi "German Christians" received Brunner's essay on natural theology with high praise. Though he would not suggest that Brunner intended to assist the Nazi movement, Barth thinks that the danger of such misuse is part of the problem with the theology Brunner proposes. Any talk about a human capacity to hear God's Word inevitably tempts us to identify our own answers with God's. Brunner cannot avoid these dangers by being more careful. The problem is inherent in the way he speaks of God and of humanity. *Wortmächtigkeit* as a human potential is merely an "empty space" which may, in fact, be filled by something other than the Word of God, something which we will then mistake for the divine commnadment that redirects our life in a new situation.[44]

After reading Brunner, Barth even concedes that his own first approaches to theology were mistaken. The dialectical despair over all political, philosophical, and "religious" solutions to the problems of the new age, Barth now sees as a kind of negative image of the self-confident nationalism of the German Christians. *The Epistle to the Romans* also sought to establish its "point of contact" between God and humanity by destroying all human systems and clearing a pathway for the Word. That strategy, too, is wrong. "That destruction of the 'fictions of *Weltanschauungen*' [worldviews] which I can with my little piece of despair undertake and carry out, is bound to issue in the erection of the worst of all idols, namely, a so-called truth from the throne of which *I* consider myself able to see through all gods and unmask them as idols."[45]

Thus Barth breaks decisively with his own early dialectical method, for that method has begun to defeat its own purpose. Instead of displacing every idol, it has made a new god of the one who smashes the idols. Any attempt to specify a starting point for thinking about God will doubtless come to the same end.

So at the conclusion of his "No!" to Brunner's orders of creation, Barth leaves us where he has left us before. We have no systematic guidance for our actions, but we are spared the danger of systematically mistaking for God that which is clearly not God. Compared to this first theological task of preserving the freedom and initiative of God, the second, missionary task of making God intelligible is misleading and dangerous. There is no *Anknüpfungspunkt* (point of contact) between God's thoughts and ours.

> The Holy Ghost . . . does not stand in need of any point of contact but that which he himself creates. Only retrospectively is it possible to reflect on the way in which he "makes contact" with a man, and this retrospect will ever be retrospect upon a miracle.[46]

We see now why the debate between Barth and Brunner fails to settle the central point at issue between them. The debate does not advance because Barth does not intend it to advance. To enter into argument over the scope of our knowledge of God is already a dangerous concession to the way of thinking that Barth opposes. Such theology, he says, is like a snake: If you allow yourself to stare at it in fascination, it will eventually strike and bite you. The only solution is to hit it and kill it as soon as you see it.[47]

Positivism and Theology

Barth's conviction that there are certain issues which cannot be debated in theology corresponds to a growing concern among philosophers at that time to distinguish questions to which our answers can be right or wrong from questions which cannot, properly speaking, be answered at all. The "Vienna Circle," a group of philosophers and scientists, insisted that the only meaningful questions are those which can be resolved by appeal to scientific verification. Questions like, Can anything travel faster than light? or Does drinking coffee increase the risk of heart attack? may be difficult to answer, but they are real questions. We know what experimental procedures and operations of logic we would have to follow to obtain an answer, and when the questions have been decisively answered, we can recognize that, too. Questions like, Does God exist? or Is pleasure truly good? are queries of a different sort. They do not yield to experimental investigation, and we suspect that no amount of evidence would conclusively settle the question one way or another.

In the aftermath of World War I, Rudolf Carnap, Moritz Schlick, the mathematician Kurt Goedel, and others of the Vienna Circle sought to comprehend the overwhelming multitude of questions facing European society by first distinguishing those that could possibly be answered from those that could not. Together with British philosophers, including Bertrand Russell and A. J. Ayer, they developed the philosophy of logical positivism during the same decade that Barth was shaping his challenge to the conventional answers of liberal theology.

While the logical positivists concerned themselves chiefly with problems of scientific investigation and mathematics, their methods had implications for ethics. The traditional questions of ethics, which turn on the nature of the good and the proper goals of human life, largely refuse to yield to investigations that a positivist could regard as decisive. Moritz Schlick, in the classic positivist work *Problems of Ethics*,[48] pointed out the implications of this problem. It does not render ethical questions unimportant, for people are still passionately concerned about the things they value and the goals they seek. It does mean that ethical problems are not the sort of problems to which we can *know* the answers. We must be content to understand as clearly as we can what persons do value and how they organize their lives to achieve their goals, but we cannot know that their values are truly consistent with their humanity, cannot say whether they should hold the values they do. Moral choice in public life, therefore, is not a matter of knowing what is best for society; it is a matter of clearly identifying which public problems have answers we can know and of minimizing the conflicts over issues which cannot be resolved.[49]

This ethical 'noncognitivism', as it came to be called, seemed to many to serve the purpose of social reconstruction by putting limits on the extravagant claims that characterized imperial ambitions in an earlier era. If we cannot truly know what constitutes the human good, then political systems that claim to possess the good, that press us into its service and impose their demands on others must be fundamentally mistaken. If we cannot, in principle, settle the differences between our different systems of values, then perhaps the appropriate political task is to find ways to live with our differences and to establish each person's right to hold an individual system of values within a framework of social cooperation. The rallying cries of crusades, inquisitions, and imperialisms are silenced once and for all by logic, for while there are no limits on what a person may assert, there are strict limits on what one can claim to know. Politicians, writers, preachers, and prophets may offer us their programs with a "take it or leave it," but they cannot demonstrate that we *must* take it. We remain logically free to follow or not, as our own values and inclinations dictate.

Barth was no doubt aware of this important movement in philosophy, and the logical positivist position that fundamental propositions in theology cannot be demonstrated to be true or false may help us to understand Bonhoeffer's remark, quoted at the beginning of this chapter, that Barth has a "positivist doctrine of revelation." Certainly Barth did not mean that the truths of faith and the commandments of God are unknowable, but that they are known only in faith, on the basis of God's Word to us. They cannot be demonstrated by any means that people use to establish the truth of their ideas scientifically. In that sense, the positivists are correct to treat propositions about God and God's commandments quite differently from the way they treat propositions about things in the world of ordinary experience—theorems of mathematics or theoretical entities like protons, electrons, and quarks in physics. Barth had insisted on that difference from the very beginning of his work in dialectical theology.

Barth is not a positivist, but he provides a theological system that is curiously compatible with the limits on argumentation set down by logical positivism. Only faith can assure us of the reality of God or validate the commandments we receive from the Word of God. Barth's insistence that the Word creates its own hearing, that there is no human capacity ready to receive it, amounts to a rejection of every argument by which one might attempt to establish the reality of a divine order in nature or even to show that the paradoxes and contradictions of our human experience can only be resolved by God. Barth's theology is sometimes criticized as "unphilosophical" because he refuses to examine the tenets of theology from any critical standpoint outside the faith. If, however, the positivists are correct, Barth is the most philosophical of theologians because he alone does not rest his case on an argument that cannot be made. "The Word of God becomes knowable by making itself knowable. The application of what has just been said to the epistemological problem consists in the fact that we hold fast to this statement and not one step beyond do we take."[50]

With that, Barth proposes to end the discussion of "natural theology," leaving Brunner with the difficult task of not only sustaining his own case, but also establishing that the argument is possible in the first place. To determine how well Brunner upholds his part of the debate, we must first decide rather carefully just what he has to do.

Barth, of course, wants to push Brunner into an *analogia entis*. He wants to put Brunner in the position of arguing in the manner of Roman Catholic natural theology from the characteristics of human beings to the characteristics of God. Then Brunner's vaunted loyalty to the reformers collapses, and one might as well, so Barth jests, knock humbly at the door of the Vatican and explain that the whole theological controversy from the Reformation onward has all been a misunderstanding.[51]

Brunner, however, has no such intention. We have already noted that his arguments in this period are largely negative, stressing the contradictions inherent in philosophical accounts of human life. He seeks to show that the Word, when we encounter it, comes to us as an answer to puzzles we knew we had but were unable to resolve for ourselves. This negative argument is hardly an *analogia entis,* and even in the most positive statement of his position in *The Divine Imperative,* Brunner never goes further than the statement that in the orders of creation man who does not know God "perceives something of the will of God."[52] The negative argument alone, however, is not sufficient. If confusion were the last word on human knowledge, Brunner really would have advanced no further than Barth's dialectic. What distinguishes his position is his appreciation of the practical side of this ungainly human intellect which trips all over itself in its attempt to discern ultimate reality. We fail miserably to explain what duty is or what good means, but we do know clearly enough what we have to do to build a factory and keep it running, to form a family and raise our children, to govern our communities and organize our life as a nation. *Wortmächtigkeit* is thus an ambiguous power. It signals at once that our words create puzzles for us words alone cannot answer *and* that in the use of words, in language and the communities that language creates we find also the power to order and sustain our lives according to a plan that seems a part of the world itself.

So the secular individual who gropes in confusion for a final explanation of moral beliefs, or a sense of purpose, or a dreadful guilt may be nonetheless a compassionate mother, or a skilled technician, or an able governor. What Brunner insists from the beginning is that in these practical tasks these persons who know nothing of God nevertheless in some real sense do God's will. That is why the people of God can enter into a public moral discussion with them, and that is what makes the forum where those discussions take place a field for the Christian's missionary task. The Word creates its own hearing, perhaps, but this for Brunner can only mean that it comes to us as the unexpected answer, which we did not propose, to questions that arise when we are about the human business that we take most seriously. If we had no useful knowledge about the state, the church, the family, work, and culture, no one would be surprised that our efforts to move beyond this technical mastery collapse in confusion. Brunner's puzzle is more profound; knowing how much we know, how is it that we can know no more?

Brunner thus avoids the attempt to know God by knowing ourselves that characterizes the *analogia entis,* but he also plainly denies Barth's *analogia fidei,* the claim that we know nothing ourselves unless we know it first in God. For Brunner to be right, there must be a general human nature which imposes requirements on our actions, which determines that, unless we act in such and such ways, we will be at cross-purposes with ourselves and our attempts to order our lives, and our relationships with others will fail. Brunner's insistence that these requirements are part of the orders of creation sets him at odds with Barth, but it also sets him against their positivist contemporaries. It is along this broader front, not over the narrowly defined issue of natural theology, that Brunner must defend his case.

He seldom does so. His attention is focused on Barth, on the denial that he has formulated an *analogia entis* or that his *Wortmächtigkeit* means anything like a literal "capacity for revelation." When he speaks of the constancies of human nature and the regular patterns that human institutions follow in the orders of creation, he treats these as commonplace observations that would appear to any observer who took the trouble to look a little below the surface of things. Yet it is at just that point that we, half a century after *The Divine Imperative,* are most apt to have problems with Brunner. The hierarchies of authority he describes in the family and the state do not seem natural and right at all to many of us, and we are far more aware than Brunner seems to have been of the multiplicity of forms under which human life has been satisfactorily organized. Just such reservations led Brunner's positivist contemporaries to conclude that anything we say in the realm of general human nature or universal norms of behavior must not claim to be knowledge, but we must have such knowledge if the possibilities *and* the limits that Brunner finds in *Wortmächtigkeit* are to mean anything at all.

It is a tribute to Barth's rhetorical skill that he kept Brunner on the defensive throughout their debate over natural theology. By forcing him to deny repeatedly that he intended any *analogia entis,* Barth kept Brunner protesting his own loyalty to the Reformation and prevented him from making a stronger case for the orders of creation. The phantom problem of Brunner's "Catholicism" dominated the argument, while the issue of Barth's affinity with the positivists remained unexplored.

To describe Barth's success here as "rhetorical" does not mean that he had no substantive point, but it is important to note how much of the force of his case against Brunner depends on the context of the time. The danger of Brunner's position is that it has been adopted by "German Christian" theologians who sympathize with Nazism. Very well, but do Brunner's ideas really serve that ideology, or is Barth blaming Brunner for the errors of his readers? Could the same complaint be made persuasively in 1924 or 1954? Or is Brunner simply charged with the evil that happens to be afoot in 1934? The danger of Brunner's position is that it is akin to Roman Catholicism. Very well, but does not that dangerous tendency, if it existed in 1934, actually make Brunner more worthy of consideration in the ecumenical era of the 1980s?

The crucial step in Brunner's ethical theory is simply the argument that there are "existing facts of human corporate life which lie at the root of all historical life as unalterable presuppositions," facts which "are unalterable in their fundamental structure and, at the same time, relate and unite men to one another in a definite way."[53] Barth and the positivists alike denied that we can know the sort of facts Brunner depends on, and that makes Brunner's argument with Barth relevant to a broader range of philosophical issues. Yet Brunner's first argument should be with the positivists on the question of what we can know, not with Barth over whether the Word of God renders such knowledge unnecessary. Because Barth presses him to defend his theology, Brunner leaves a crucial first step unguarded. He treats the orders of creation as an assumption, a commonly agreed upon starting point, a fact about humanity that is obvious to all. Only, if this first step is not obvious, then Barth has won the debate by default, for there would be no alternative to his "theological positivism" as a starting point for ethics. By drawing Brunner into extended debate on our knowledge of God, Barth avoids having to defend his own position on our knowledge of humanity.

Brunner's assumptions about the orders of creation may seem strange to twentieth-century positivism and problematic even to late twentieth-century common sense, but his position is consistent with most of the Christian tradition before him. However much theologians have differed over our natural ability to know God, most of them have agreed that we can establish the general requirements of human life and organize the practical tasks these requirements impose without immediate dependence on divine assistance. This realism or ethical naturalism provides the basis for a public discussion between theology and nontheological knowledge, and it is this realism that links Brunner to the broad stream of Christian thought concerned with natural law. To that extent, perhaps, his interests are "Catholic," but we must not interpret that Catholicism in Barth's way, as a static, Tridentine dogma that never changes. Rather, we must now explore Brunner's affinity to another historic faith that was seeking its own new path after World War I.

NOTES

1. Dietrich Bonhoeffer, *Letters and Papers from Prison*, ed. Eberhard Bethge (New York: Macmillan Co., 1971), 286. We will see later in more detail what Bonhoeffer meant when he called Barth's work a "positivist" doctrine of revelation.

2. Quoted in John Baillie, ed., *Natural Theology* (London: Geoffrey Bles, 1946), 11.

3. Barth, *The Holy Ghost,* 81.

4. Brunner, *Divine Imperative.*

5. Ibid., 210.

6. Ibid., 263.

7. Ibid., 337.

8. Barth, *Epistle* 517.

9. Brunner, *Divine Imperative,* 214.

10. Ibid., 272.

11. Ibid., 398.

12. Ibid., 433–34.

13. Emil Brunner, *Justice and the Social Order,* trans. Mary Hottinger (New York: Harper & Brothers, 1945), 128–29. Brunner completed his manuscript of this work in 1943.

14. Idem, *Divine Imperative,* 56.

15. Ibid., 350.

16. Ibid., 416.

17. Ibid., 474.

18. Ibid.

19. Gustavo Gutiérrez, *A Theology of Liberation,* trans. Caridad Inda and John Eagleson (Maryknoll, N.Y.: Orbis Books, 1973).

20. On the importance of social analysis in liberation theology, see Juan Luis Segundo, *The Liberation of Theology,* trans. John Drury (Maryknoll, N.Y.: Orbis Books, 1976); and James Cone, "Christian Faith and Political Praxis," in *The Challenge of Liberation Theology,* ed. Brian Mahan and L. Dale Richesin (Maryknoll, N.Y.: Orbis Books, 1981), 52–64.

21. Aristotle, *Nicomachean Ethics,* trans Martin Ostwald (Indianapolis: Bobbs-Merrill, 1962), 221–23.

22. Brunner, *Divine Imperative,* 374.

23. Idem, *Justice,* 69.

24. Idem, *Divine Imperative,* 371–73.

25. Idem, *Justice,* 69.

26. Rosemary Ruether, *New Woman/New Earth* (New York: Seabury Press, 1975).

27. Reinhold Niebuhr, *Faith and History* (New York: Charles Scribner's Sons, 1949), 173–84.

28. Idem, "Liberty and Equality," in *Pious and Secular America* (New York: Charles Scribner's Sons, 1958), 61–85.

29. Brunner, *Divine Imperative,* 433–37.

30. Andre Bieler, *The Social Humanism of Calvin* (Richmond, Va.: John Knox Press, 1964), 33.

31. Brunner, *Divine Imperative,* 437.

32. See chapter 2, 24–28.

33. Brunner, *Divine Imperative,* 43.

34. Idem, *Justice,* 127.

35. Especially T. H. Green (1836–1882), F. H. Bradley (1846–1924), and Hastings Rashdall (1858–1924).

36. Both essays are published in English in Baillie, *Natural Theology.*

37. For the distinction between "normative ethics" and "metaethics" see chapter 2, 36.

38. Gen. 1:27.

39. Brunner put it more precisely by saying that the *material* image of God was destroyed by sin, but the *formal* image remains in *Wortmächtigkeit*. See Baillie, *Natural Theology,* 23–24.

40. Emil Brunner, *Man in Revolt,* trans. Olive Wyon (Philadelphia: Westminster Press, 1939), 114–18.

41 Ibid., 116.

42. Ibid., 116–17.

43. Paul Lehmann, "Barth and Brunner: The Dilemma of the Protestant Mind," *Journal of Religion,* 20 (1940): 137.

44. Barth, *Church Dogmatics,* 1/1: 278.

45. Idem, "No!" in Baillie, *Natural Theology,* 120.

46. Ibid., 121.

47. Ibid., 76.

48. Moritz Schlick, *Problems of Ethics,* trans. David Rynin (New York: Prentice-Hall, 1939).

49. See, for example, Felix Oppenheim, *Moral Principles in Political Philosophy,* 2d ed. (New York: Random House, 1976), 144–84.

50. Barth, *Church Dogmatics,* 1/1: 282.

51. Idem, "No!", 95.

52. Brunner, *Divine Imperative,* 221.

53. Ibid., 210.

4
REASON
AND RESISTANCE

The unity of faith and reason was a principal theme of European theology in the nineteenth century. Confronted with growing skepticism about the claims of religious orthodoxy, theologians often sought to show that the underlying meaning of dogma was compatible with the leading philosophical ideas of the day. This impulse to unite the truths of faith and reason in a new synthesis was felt especially where discoveries in science and new ways of studying human society challenged traditional doctrines concerning nature and human communities. In France, the Catholic "modernist" movement rejected the formality of Scholastic theology and subordinated doctrinal questions to practical issues of life in the church. British theologians initiated an Anglican modernism to meet the challenge of Darwin's evolutionary theory and to adapt the faith to new discoveries in science. German Protestants, especially, combined a new, critical examination of the origins of Christianity with a confidence that the Hegelian view of history would replace any unwarranted assumptions about divine intervention at the beginning of the faith with an assured, expectable conclusion to the historical process.

In Germany, this synthetic approach became the theological counterpart to the political "union of throne and altar" that characterized cooperation between the monarchy and the Protestant state churches, and it threatened to destroy the churches along with the monarchy in the aftermath of World War I. The ill-fated alliance of Protestant theology with the Prussian state prompted Barth to rethink the whole relationship between faith and reason and led him to the dialectical theology that rejects any attempt at synthesis.

We have already noted, however, that this union of Protestantism and imperialism which so offended Barth was not the only theological response available. In place of an expectation based on the convergence of Christianity and culture in history, it is possible to link Christian faith with a realistic, reasoned assessment of human needs and goals that unite persons across social barriers and national boundaries. That link between faith and culture may then hearten persons whose efforts to transform society would otherwise seem hopeless and strengthen the resistance of those who protest repressive regimes out of loyalty to a wider humanity. Barth is right, of course, that we may avoid the evils of a static, self-glorifying synthesis of faith and culture by rigorously excluding the point of contact between God's commands and human knowledge; but then we also lose the power of theological realism to bring about a criticism of the existing society that encourages social transformation.

Within this transformative approach, we must include the ethics of Emil Brunner. Despite the weaknesses we noted in his theory of "critical cooperation," Brunner's aim is clearly to uphold the order of creation as a permanent standard by which any particular historical order can be judged. The union of faith and reason is achieved when the task of ordering society that we share with all other persons takes on for Christians the serious aspect that it is also cooperation with the perfecting work of God.

Our task in this chapter is to consider Brunner's "critical cooperation" in relationship to another form of theological realism, Roman Catholic natural law ethics. Despite the lack of sympathy between Protestants and Roman Catholics so evident in the Barth-Brunner debate over natural theology, the two major Christian groups faced the immense problems of defeat, depression, and dictatorship in common, and they emerged from World War II determined that their historic rivalry, which had helped Hitler to divide and conquer them, should not govern their relationships in the future.

One of the most significant elements in this new cooperation has been the Protestants' appreciation of the importance of natural law theory in wartime resistance to totalitarianism and in guiding the reconstruction of society.[1] Because of the importance of this development for Protestant ethics in the last half of the twentieth century, it is necessary to shift our attention from Barth's narrowly focused debate with Brunner over the "point of contact" between God and humanity. We must instead attempt to establish our own point of contact between the Protestant attempt to find a faith adequate to the social challenges after World War I and the Roman Catholic adaptation of an old theological synthesis to that quite new social reality.

Catholicism and Natural Law

Catholic natural law theory brings a critical perspective to observations of society because it insists that human life is ordered toward certain basic goals. Customs, rules, and conventions may vary from place to place and time to time, but the fundamental aims of human life remain constant, and in every time and place they give shape to social institutions. The law that governs this common development is natural in two senses. First, it is part of nature and not the product of custom or the result of human choice. Second, it can be known by all persons. No faith or special revelation is required to discern its basic requirements, and lack of faith does not excuse one from knowing and following the natural order. Those outside of the faith cannot be expected to understand the sacrament of baptism, for example, and a non-Christian ruler who tried to make laws to regulate baptism would probably do a very bad job of the matter. All persons, however, are able to understand the basic requirements of honesty and the need to refrain from harming their neighbors. Rulers, Christian or not, should put these natural law precepts into force, and they may properly be accused of failing in their duty if they do not. A synthesis between the reasoned moral principles of society and the moral precepts of Christianity is thus presupposed, and a ruler who fails in respect of the one has also failed in respect of the other.

Historically speaking, the most important statement of this natural law theory is found in the writings of Thomas Aquinas (1225?–1274), the Dominican theologian whose *Summa Theologica* provides a systematic treatment of the major theological issues of the Middle Ages.[2] Aquinas used Aristotelian philosophy to systematize widely held Christian ideas about the moral law. In the early centuries of Christianity, religious, legal, and philosophical ideas combined to provide an idea of a universal system of moral requirements that all persons could know and follow. Despite the variety of cultures, religions, and customs in the ancient world, Christians could point to Paul's testimony that the Gentiles carry out the essential precepts of God's law "by the light of nature,"[3] and to the common idea in Roman law of a *ius gentium,* a "law of the nations," that unites all peoples in observing basic moral requirements of honesty and promise keeping and that universally forbids murder, theft, and violence. Stoic philosophers explained these regularities through their concept of reason, or *logos,* which is both the fundamental structure of reality and the form of rationality which all persons share. Christians and Jews adapted this *logos* concept to their own idea of a creator God who made all things and is present to all persons. From the first, then, Christian thinkers adapted and spread ideas of basic human moral obligations that applied in all ages and cultures. Thomas Aquinas' achievement was to systematize these ideas and place them in a comprehensive philosophical and theological framework.

Aquinas located the ultimate source of order in the universe in the *eternal law,* the divine reason which governs all things and supplies the constancy that the regularities of nature and of the moral life require. While only the blessed, the Christian saints who have attained to an understanding of the essence of God, can fully know this eternal law, every rational creature has some knowledge of what this law requires. "For every knowledge of truth is a kind of reflection and participation of the eternal law, which is the unchangeable truth, as Augustine says."[4] Hence even those who do not acknowledge the truth of the Christian faith are not excluded from knowledge of basic moral requirements, for the general principles of morality may be seen everywhere. In subsequent moral theology, the *natural law* acquired the precise denotation of those universal moral precepts which could be known by reason alone, without consulting biblical revelation or relying on any special divine assistance.

Aristotle and Aquinas specifically agreed that the reason which all persons share should govern and direct their desires and their other natural powers. It is by reason that we know the proper ends toward which human life and all the things human beings can use are directed. Reason links us to reality by indicating the possibilities and limits that nature imposes on all our activities. It tells us what we can do and warns us what we cannot do without distorting our own lives and our relations with others. Hence the idea of natural law provides the basis for a consensus on the requirements for human law in a good society. Reason can determine the good apart from a theological warrant, although Christians can act with the special confidence that what reason rightly discerns is, in fact, "a kind of reflection and participation of the eternal law." The laws that particular societies make for themselves, then, should reflect a reasoned decision about what the natural law requires. Human law, rightly understood, participates in natural law, just as the natural law participates in the eternal.

After Aquinas, however, Catholic moral theology took a rather different direction. Pursuit of the good, later writers suggested, is motivated chiefly by God's grace, while the natural moral law serves the negative function of restraining the evil desires which grace has not yet overcome. The chief object of rational moral inquiry, then, is to determine whether an act is permissible, not to discover the good. "Casuistry," as it came to be called, developed into an elaborate system of reasoning to apply moral principles to particular cases in order to determine whether an action is morally correct. When this way of thinking was applied to the practice of private confession and penance, it produced a very extensive collection of "Manuals," or guides to moral theology, for priests hearing confessions. This literature no doubt helped bring uniformity to Catholic morals in Europe and provided much reassurance for troubled consciences. Nevertheless, the emphasis on deciding whether or not a particular act is wrong gave a legalistic and negative character to Catholic ethics, especially after the Council of Trent (1545–1563.)[5]

Moral Theology Since Leo XIII

Important efforts to relieve this legalism and emphasize the positive goals of the moral life were made early in the nineteenth century, but it was not until 1879, when Pope Leo XIII decreed that the theology of Thomas Aquinas should be the foundation for the training of Roman Catholic clergy, that a renewed appreciation of the role of natural law in defining common goals for human society was possible. We must not suppose that the Catholic moral theologians who stressed Thomistic responses to the social and political crises of the twentieth century were simply reasserting an ancient system, oblivious to new realities. No less than Barth or Brunner, the Catholic theologians of the 1920s believed that the theology and ethics of a previous generation were inadequate to the demands of the new situation. Their uses of natural law were attempts to recover truths that had been ignored or half-forgotten in Catholic moral theology, and their turn to ancient sources was at the same time a search for new directions. What distinguished them from their Protestant counterparts was that the Thomistic tradition to which they turned placed great trust in human reason for solutions to the problems of justice and the social order. Thomas' idea that all persons have some knowledge of eternal divine wisdom and that all are capable of regulating their conduct by that knowledge contrasts sharply with Barth's dismissal of human moral categories or Brunner's inventory of the failures of philosophical ethics. Catholic theologians were no less critical of previous systems, but they had more confidence that theologians, philosophers, jurists, and diplomats working together could devise new answers adequate to the new situation.

One important instance of this cooperation was the use of philosophical phenomenology by a number of Catholic writers. The philosopher Edmund Husserl (1859–1938) used the term 'phenomenology' to name a method of investigation that seeks to resolve philosophical problems by careful attention to immediate human experience. The phenomenologist tries to describe what is directly present to consciousness in an experience without regard to the usual scientific explanations of how that experience happens or what is "really" there in the world. Husserl largely confined his inquiries to our awareness of ordinary objects in space and time, but others quickly extended the method to less concrete experiences. Max Scheler (1874–1928) found in phenomenology an alternative both to the positivists' reduction of ethics to individual preferences and to formalized systems of ethics which tried to deduce all moral judgments from a single goal (teleology) or a universal rule of action (deontology). Scheler thought that a phenomenological explanation would show that values of various sorts are real elements in experience. Values of pleasure, aesthetic values, experiences of holiness, and an immediate awareness of moral right and wrong are all present in the world of experience. They are realities which can be dismissed only by a "scientific" outlook which oversimplifies reality by reducing it to a world of material interactions. A system of ethics adequate to human experience will begin with these values, not with a system of rules or goals imposed on experience.[6]

Although he rejected Catholic Christianity in 1922, Scheler was active in the church during his most important philosophical work, and he influenced many younger theologians through his lectures at the time and later through his writing. One of them, Karol Wojtyla, has become Pope John Paul II. Another was Dietrich von Hildebrand, author of widely used texts on Catholic moral theology.[7] What these theologians found in Scheler was an approach to ethics that allowed for a careful restatement of basic human values in the context of modern experience, while it provided some assurance that these values are indeed universal, part of the structure of reality and knowable by all persons, just as Thomas Aquinas said they should be. The phenomeno-logical method remains an important part of contemporary Catholic moral theology.[8]

Perhaps more important for our study are the Catholic philosphers and political theorists who followed the lead of Leo XIII and applied the renewed interest in Thomism to the search for an appropriate modern political order. While few could seriously propose to recreate the medieval society Thomas had known, his careful delineation of the relationships between the eternal law, natural law, and human law suggested an appropriate relationship between the various powers that order human life in society. Protestants tended in the manner of Emil Brunner to see social life organized in a set of discrete, separate orders. Thomistic thought stressed the unity of human life, the pervasive influence of familial, social, and religious communities on all aspects of human existence. Moreover, while Protestants usually saw the orders as fundamentally equal in power and importance, ranged as it were horizontally alongside one another, Catholic writers thought of the ends and purposes served by different communities as hierarchical, ranged vertically, with the purposes of religious community, for exam-ple, clearly outranking those concerned only with human society and its good.

What the Thomistic hierarchy of eternal law, natural law, and human law suggested was a way of understanding the hierarchy of communities that minimized conflict between them. Communities which seem to serve very different purposes may become involved in vicious competition unless they have a way of understanding their goals as complementary. Religious communities in particular tend to claim an exclusive loyalty that sets them at odds with other allegiances to family or to the state, especially when these latter communities also press strong claims for themselves. It helps, of course, if the com-munities can agree that their goals are clearly different, so that the family and the state are not competing for control of childrearing, for example, or so that the state does not infringe unduly on the produc-tive functions of the economic community. Something like this insight undergirds the Protestant attempt to sharply distinguish the various orders of creation and to assign each its legitimate function. The hierarchy of eternal law, natural law, and human law suggests a further possibility. It may be that these functions are not only different, but when they are divided in a proper fashion, they may be related so that the more important, "higher" functions can include the "lower" with-out disrupting them. Just as the human law should conform to natural law—although not all of natural law can or should be made into human law—and just as natural law forms a part, though not all of the eternal law, so it should be that every goal human beings seek in a good political society not only serves their worldly interests, it also prepares them better to seek the spiritual good that leads ultimately to direct awareness of the eternal law.

The implications of this are twofold. First, Christians can and should participate in the improvement of society because living in a good society makes them better fit for the distinctly religious tasks that take them beyond society's goals. Second, in working for a better society, Christians need not be especially concerned whether their partners in that enterprise share their specific Christian convictions. Those who seek a better society for its own sake, provided that they seek it rightly, following their own insights into natural law, will create the same social order that the Christians also seek as a means to higher purposes.

This hierarchical alternative to the Protestants' distribution of social functions among the various orders of creation is most fully articulated in the works of Jacques Maritain,[9] but the idea is also present in Catholic thought about the purpose and limits of the state during the period in which German theologians in particular had to wrestle with the problems of democracy and dictatorship. At that time, the work of Catholic jurists and diplomats, notably Heinrich Rommen,[10] was as important as that of the theologians. The proper functioning of the state, according to these theorists, is assured not by an authority who maintains order, but by conformity to a natural law. That law, in turn, is something which all persons, not just those in authority, can know.

Reason and the Orders of Creation

With this overview of developments in Roman Catholic moral theology, we can proceed to a closer consideration of the orders of creation and their relationship to natural law. In the last chapter, we saw that thinking in terms of the orders of creation entails more confidence in human reason than Barth was willing to allow. Part of the rhetorical strategy of Barth's "No!" was to depict the characteristic human capacity for the word as a dangerous foothold for pride and self-deception, a power that would soon be used to claim direct human knowledge of God and to hallow a self-centered view of the world. Brunner's claim that thoughtful work in the world is at the same time a way of working in the kingdom of God appears from Barth's perspective to be an extravagant estimate of human powers.

Taken on his own terms, however, Brunner is ambivalent about reason, and when we compare his position with the Catholic natural law theorists, he seems more inclined to dwell on the limitations of reason. Brunner makes much of human success in practical tasks—forming families, maintaining law, producing goods, and the like—but he is skeptical of our ability to fully explain what we do. Side by side with the success of family life, legal processes, and factory production, we have the failure of psychology, philosophy, and economic theory to explain these activities fully. Technical reason accomplishes life's tasks better than speculative or theoretical reason understands them. As Brunner's treatment of philosophical ethics in *Man in Revolt* indicates,[11] attempts to give a theoretical account of basic human choices are always incomplete and often contradictory. This is not to suggest that reason is a feeble power that we could just as well do without. "The Creator has not endowed us with reason simply as a present," Brunner says, "but as the essential core of life, and this is His Will."[12] Nevertheless, reason is limited. Reason serves human purposes, and its powers are limited by that use. We reason not to know the world as God knows it, but to understand it rightly as a field for human action. If we forget this, Brunner suggests, we will waste our energy on theories that claim to tell us more than they can know, and the theories themselves will disintegrate in controversy or self-contradiction.

Respecting the limits of reason means that we must recognize the intimate links between reason and imagination. Brunner adopts an Augustinian theme popular among Protestant writers that contrasts sharply with the Thomist view that reason's principal function is to give us an accurate account of the world as it is. Brunner links the concept of reason to creative, active freedom.[13] Reason would be of little use unless it included the capacity to envision what might be as well as to know what is. Because reason enables us to see unrealized possibilities in reality, the artist can create what no one has yet seen, and the researcher can design experiments that add to the scope of our knowledge. Because reason frees us from the limits of what is given, even the most oppressed worker and the least educated child cannot be confined in the limits society has imposed on them. Their humanity alone insures that they know things could be otherwise. "This freedom is the life element, indeed, if one may venture to put it so, it is the real substance of reason; without this freedom to raise himself in free self-determination above what is given, man, as man, cannot be imagined."[14]

Brunner's concern has important implications for ethics. It is easy to treat freedom primarily as a problem for law and government, so that the question becomes how much latitude the state will allow its citizens to think, write, and publish criticisms of the political *status quo*. If it is the government that properly decides how much freedom we have, we may not like the decision, but we have few grounds on which to criticize it. Christian thinking about freedom, therefore, must begin instead with a freedom which is essential to human life itself and which cannot be conferred or revoked by any act of government. "Man is older than the State," as Leo XIII put it, "and he holds the right of providing for the life of his body prior to the formation of any State."[15] This concern is often expressed in general terms of human rights or human dignity. Brunner attempts to specify it by identifying a primary human freedom that begins with consciousness itself. The inescapable freedom that consciousness confers provides the foundation for every particular freedom we may claim from the state.

To identify this freedom of consciousness as the "real substance" of reason, however, diminishes the importance of reason as the power that discloses the limits reality imposes on us. The tradition of Aristotle and Thomas Aquinas identifies reason as the power that understands the ultimate purposes of things, so that reason assesses momentary desires in the light of a permanent concept of human nature and the human good. Brunner's idea of reason, by contrast, expands the meaning of reason, but he limits its critical, controlling role in human affairs.

For Brunner, reason's special role is in the order of culture.[16] Science, education, and the arts are the domain of reason because there the foundational freedom of consciousness is expressed in forms that can be shared and studied, and the works of one generation can be passed on to the next. Of course, from a certain perspective the construction of a solid bridge (the order of labor) or the management of an effective court system (the order of the state) is as creative as drama and sculpture. In the order of culture, however, people create representations of life in which the difference that reason discerns between what is and what might be becomes the basis for an expression in words or form or color that helps persons locate their lives in the world and understand forces which before they could not comprehend. The works of culture are rational in Brunner's terms because they are products of freedom of consciousness which never is bound to accept the world the way it is and which can always combine the elements of experience in new ways. Poems, plays, and paintings are rational because they come from that freedom which is "the real substance of reason," but it is almost beside the point to ask if they are also *true*. Where reason marks the difference between vision and reality, ordinary measures of truth—accuracy, correspondence to reality, clear and unambiguous expression—do not apply.

Problems in Brunner's Approach

All this sounds rather like the positivist argument that terms like 'true' and 'false' do not apply to statements of human choice and aspiration. Brunner would no doubt reject the association. He had less sympathy than Barth for his philosphical contemporaries who moved with the Vienna Circle. At the same time, however, his quarrel with Barth over natural law kept him from fully developing the implications of his reliance on the orders of creation. In these early works, Brunner is a rationalist, but he does not fully develop a realist alternative to positivism. He does not rely on reason to tell him how the world really is, and indeed he distrusts all theories because they are one-sided presentations that cannot completely account for the political, psychological, or moral experience they represent.

For Brunner, the command of God cannot be heard in the constructions of reason. His criticism of natural law theory is precisely that it replaces attentiveness to the command of God with a reasoned inquiry into the human good.

> According to the definition of the Aristotelian-Thomistic school of thought, for instance, the principle of the Good, objectively, is not the will of God, and subjectively, obedience to this will, but it is "adaptation to the nature of man." The Good is "all that brings man's nature to perfection."[17]

Brunner's insistence here on the metaethic of the will of God reiterates the fundamental position that links him to Barth's enterprise from the beginning, but he misunderstands the hierarchical principle of Catholic moral theology when he suggests that the natural law theorists *replace* the divine will with an idea of human good. Rather, Catholic thought regards reason's moral conclusions as valid precisely because the natural law discerned by reason is a "kind of reflection and participation of the eternal law." The will of God remains the final source of moral—and all other—truth. Reason's important place in ethics rests on its power to know a natural order that is ordered by the divine will. That, in itself, is not so different from Brunner's understanding of the orders of creation. The real difference between Brunner and the Catholics is not over what 'good' means, but over the power of reason to know the good.

The Catholic confidence in reason in ethics quickly runs up against the ambiguities and disagreements that pervade all real moral problems. It is easy to speak theoretically about a reasoned morality, but the persistence of questions about the morality of warfare or capital punishment, for example, are reminders that apparently reasonable positions may elicit equally reasonable objections. Similarly, the difficulty of knowing in individual cases whether someone lied about a situation or merely failed to give all the available information points to the problem of applying reasonable moral rules to specific, complicated situations. Aristotle long ago observed that in matters of ethics, we must not demand more precision than the subject will allow.[18] Catholic moral theology has generally acknowledged his point in a distinction between practical reason, which makes the always ambiguous decisions about what to do in particular cases, and speculative reason, which gives a more precise theoretical account of how the world is and what the first principles of morality are. With this reservation, however, the Thomistic natural law theory holds that reason can achieve a complete, adequate, and accurate knowledge of all that is essential to sound moral judgment.

The theoretical confusions in ethics which Brunner describes reflect the failures of individual theorists (who might, of course, have profited from a closer study of the *Summa Theologica*), but they do not indicate shortcomings in reason itself. Catholic moral theology insists that reason gives us intellectual mastery of reality for the same reason that Protestants have often sought to deny it: to preserve the command of God. Where the Protestant fears that confidence in reason will lead to excessive reliance on human powers, the Catholic argues that reason's knowledge of reality is a fundamental feature of God's creation. To reduce reason to an unrealistic idealism or an inaccurate reproduction of sense experience is to deny the power that God the Creator continues to hold over even sinful humanity, enabling them to guide their lives by reason and to know, despite their own denials, what the Creator requires of them.

Brunner, by contrast, seems to suggest that reason is a visionary power, too ready to ignore the reality of human sin and leap to a theoretical utopia which could never be realized in the world of self-centered and weak-willed persons in which we really have to live. The constraints that reason imposes in Catholic moral theology must be found, for Brunner, in experience within the orders themselves. At least that is one way to interpret his enigmatic statement that the divine imperative cannot be understood without a knowledge of the orders.[19]

By this insistence on an experiential, historical approach to God's command, Brunner seeks to avoid both the moral anarchy that would follow from absolute trust in each individual's moral judgment and the legalism that might result from insisting that what reason dictates is always right. In place of rationalism and individualism, Brunner offers a functional standard of judgment. What God commands appears in the orders of creation in terms of what we must do to keep the orders working. Such requirements can never be known with scientific precision. Indeed, they may change somewhat over time, but over time, too, collective human experience will give us a fairly detailed picture of how we must act to preserve the family or the orders of labor and culture or the state. For sinful human beings, this cumulative experience is to be trusted above any individual judgment, however sincere, and above any rational criterion, however theoretically elegant.

This careful, historical accumulation of practical wisdom no doubt occasionally contradicts other, more immediate experiences of moral obligation. The demands of conscience, the promptings of Christian love, even an individual reading of the Bible may move us to do things that defy the requirements of the orders. The child who quietly ignores a parental command that seems unjust and the citizen who resists a law that is arbitrary or discriminatory might both appeal to a sense of personal duty or to love for those who would otherwise suffer as a reason to suspend the normal lines of authority within the family or the state. Brunner insists, however, that love and conscience taken by themselves are not good guides for social action. However well they may direct us in personal, face-to-face relationships, we must test these insights against the requirement that they keep the orders functioning before we act on them in society.

> "The order" is therefore the actual theological category of the ethic of society as such, thus—from the theological point of view—it is that which distinguishes life in society from the personal relation between the "I" and the "Thou", or rather, it is that through which that personal relation receives its particular modification by society.[20]

Failure to consider the requirements of order, attempts to act directly on personal moral reason—these are wrong for Brunner because they threaten to wreck the institutions that sustain the fabric of society in which those direct, personal moral relationships become possible. The knowledge we need to act wisely regarding social problems simply is not available to individual reason, which can only envision possibilities in freedom before becoming stuck in its own web of contradictory theories. The knowledge we need is only available in the workings of the orders themselves.

We have already seen in chapter 3 that Brunner's stress on preserving the orders makes it very difficult for him to conceive of a legitimate reason to revolt against one's government. The comparison of the orders of creation doctrine with natural law theory helps us understand why this is so. The state we have, however far it may be from the perfection God intends, is nonetheless for Brunner the only school we have for learning God's will for the state. If our state is disordered and tyrannical, unable to maintain right relationships to other orders of creation, then the lessons we learn may be mostly negative, but without the concrete, historical experience of that state and the order that keeps it functioning, we have no guidance at all. Neither individual moral insight nor theories of justice and politics can tell us what to do. When we overthrow the state, we also eliminate the only source of reliable knowledge about the state.

Brunner's doubts about revolution made sense as a reflection on German politics in the years after World War I. Brunner observed the German scene from Switzerland, unlike Barth, whose academic career involved him directly in the politics of the Weimar Republic, but Brunner shared the alarm of constitutional parties like Barth's Social Democrats over the growth of conservative and radical groups who were committed to destroy the German state and replace it with an order designed according to their own political and economic theories.

As an answer to the utopians and revolutionaries of the 1920s, Brunner's insistence on principles of government shaped by actual political experience made sense. The test of a theory in ethics, however, must be its applicability to a variety of situations, and it is unclear how the stress on order in *The Divine Imperative* should speak to Christian discontent with Hitler's Reich in the 1930s or to the aspirations of those who live under oppressive dictatorships of the left or the right today. In contrast to the political and economic chaos that followed the First World War, Hitler provided plenty of order. The economy was stabilized, political disturbances were suppressed, and the trains, as the saying goes, ran on time.

Reason and Resistance

During the struggle between anti-Nazi Christians and the Nazi government, foreign observers often noted that Protestants and Catholics offered quite different explanations for their opposition and its meaning. The Protestant stance was usually confessional, resting on the integrity of the Christian message and demanding the freedom of the church to order its own life and proclaim its own message. The Catholic position, by contrast, was stated in more general terms. It rested on a natural law theory of justice and right rule and insisted that all persons, regardless of religious confession, had a moral obligation to uphold those standards.[21]

While Protestantism is usually thought to be the faith of individual conscience and resistance to arbitrary power, the Catholic teaching that every person has a basic knowledge of the natural moral law also led to striking cases of individual witness. Protestants might know Luther's conscientious "Here I stand," but they could not ignore his equally firm insistence that bad government is a punishment to be endured and bad laws may not be resisted. Catholics, by contrast, could argue that they had an individual moral obligation to assess the state's political demands in terms laid down by the natural law and an equally important obligation to act on the conclusions of their moral reasoning.[22] Aquinas observed that no one is freed from the bond of conscience by the obligation to obey a superior. "For each is bound to examine his actions according to the knowledge he has from God, whether natural, acquired, or infused."[23]

It would be too simple to explain obedience and resistance exclusively along confessional lines. Protestants, too, suffered for their opposition to Hitler, and as we shall see, some found ways to justify taking their opposition to the point of revolutionary resistance. Catholics could excuse failure to act on moral conclusions on grounds of prudence and the need to preserve public peace. Indeed, church authorities used those reasons to urge Catholics to cooperate and avoid persecution. Nevertheless, it is important to note that reliance on natural law reasoning marks a path of moral opposition to governmental power that seems to be blocked in Brunner's early accounts of the orders of creation. Where God's will is known only by understanding the orders, a reasoned judgment that the authorities are wrong cannot, strictly speaking, be real knowledge. Indeed, where the state successfully controls all channels of political information and communication, practical alternatives to the present order are hardly conceivable, and all opposition becomes utopian. Brunner's early account of the state is well-suited to protect a weak democracy from idealistic revolutionaries, but it also renders a strong totalitarianism impervious to democratic protests.

Brunner, of course, could not have known in detail of the struggles of the German resistance after 1939, but he was aware as the years passed of the limitations on his earlier position that the will of God for society is known only by understanding the state as an order of creation. In *Justice and the Social Order,* he suggested that if resistance to a totalitiarian state could be justified, that justification would rest "solely on the law of nature."[24] It will be worth closer investigation to see how this change in Brunner's thinking took shape.

Natural law provides a rule of reason against which the laws of a state can be measured. In Aquinas' hierarchical ordering, written laws have authority because they conform to the natural law, which is in turn part of the eternal law of God. The work of judges and legislators is law precisely because it connects our courts, government programs, and legal rules of action to a larger, more permanent reality that is governed by natural and divine law. The implication of this view is that rules which do not make this connection, which call for actions that violate the justice of natural law, are "laws" in appearance only. They cannot really be laws, and they cannot, therefore, claim the obligatory force that a proper law has. Similarly, rulers, lawgivers, or for that matter modern parliamentary legislatures are what they seem only when their laws are just. The power to compel obedience may remain with them long after justice departs, but at that point they have no more moral authority than a band of brigands. This implication is clear, and Catholic writers from Augustine onward have not hesitated to draw it.[25]

This could and often did lead to the conclusion that an unjust law need not be obeyed. Since the sort of authority that makes unjust law is also usually quite harsh on disobedience, most moral theologians hastened to add that an unjust law is not binding "in conscience." We may evade it or violate it or ignore it, unless, of course, our action causes other evils to occur. For example, our families may suffer persecution, or public order may be undermined. In those cases, even an unjust law may require our obedience, and we must be willing to suffer considerable injustice to ourselves before we put the public order at risk.[26] Clearly then, the occasions when justice requires us not only to disobey but to go further and actively to resist the authority that issues the unjust command will be rare indeed, but the possibility of resistance is implicit in the power to judge that a law is not really law and that an unjust lawgiver has no legitimate power. Reasonable people will hedge that possibility with extensive constraints, but the power of reason to make the judgment is never in doubt in the natural law tradition.

Historically, Protestants have approached these questions in a quite different way. Their positions have been shaped perhaps as much by events as by a commitment to a particular theory of morals, but they have consistently tried to avoid the potential conflict that the Thomists perceived between right as apprehended by reason and right as determined by the laws of the state. "The law of nature must claim no binding force for itself if the legal security of the state is to remain unshaken. That is the point at which the Reformers diverged most widely from the view of medieval Catholicism."[27]

Hence Luther was a forceful spokesman for the authority of the state. He refused to permit resistance to rulers and counseled obedience even when he thought the ruler was clearly in the wrong. It will not do for the subject to substitute a personal judgment for the authoritative decision of the ruler. When the ruler's command directly contravenes the Word of God, then disobedience is in order, but even then the refusal to obey must not lead to active resistance.

Luther's theological endorsement of secular authority and his rejection of active resistance continued even in the case of rulers who were hostile to the Reformation. Given the consistent pressure of the Holy Roman Empire against the lesser rulers who supported Luther, his movement might have disappeared from Germany altogether had he not changed his position in 1539 to allow his princely supporters to take up arms against their Emperor.[28]

Luther's reasons, however, were as significant as his action. He was persuaded by a careful lawyer's brief that the laws of the Empire themselves permitted subordinate princes to disobey and even to resist a superior who was acting without lawful authority. Luther explained his earlier prohibition of resistance by "the fact that we did not know that the governing authority's law itself grants the right of armed resistance."[29]

This limitation of resistance to authority to forms established by the authority's own law appears also in Calvinism, which assigns to the "lesser magistrates" the duty of restraining or even removing a tyrannical ruler. Calvin himself seems to approve this action only where the laws explicitly provide for such magistrates—"as in ancient times the ephors were set against the Spartan kings, or the tribunes of the people against the Roman consuls."[30] Other writers suggested that all states implicitly provide this office whether their laws say so or not. Both theologians and jurists argued that when people come together to form a state, they reserve for themselves the right to demand justice from their ruler, and the people may revoke their original agreement if the ruler begins to act outside the law.[31]

Protestants and Catholics alike, then, faced the challenges of totalitarianism in the 1930s with a history of ethical reflection on the problem of resistance to authority. In each tradition, there was a carefully graded sequence of responses from prudent obedience to a refusal to obey to active resistance against the power that issues the law. In each, the recognized right to resist in extreme cases was carefully hedged by qualifications and restrictions that insured that actual instances of resistance would be quite rare and should be undertaken only as a last resort.

These similarities in practice, however, conceal an important difference in theory. Where the Catholic natural law theory rests on a moral judgment which is in principle open to all, the Protestant constitutional theory looks to the law of the state itself to authorize resistance. Luther's explanation of 1530 is telling: "We did not know that the governing authority's law itself grants the right of armed resistance." The judgment here is not a moral conclusion which falls within the competence of theologians and philosophers and rests on fundamental principles that anyone might be expected to know. The judgment concerns technical matters of imperial and canon law which even the leaders of the Reformation were not embarrassed to admit that they did not know until the legal experts told them. It was not a mistake concerning natural law or the law of God that let Luther insist at first that the ruler must not be resisted even when his commands are wrong. On that point, Luther thought himself quite correct. What he learned was simply that the laws of *this* Empire, with its structure of federated kingdoms and principalities, permit a resistance that the biblical authorities did not envision, so that holding a ruler accountable for his injustices can be seen as part of the respect for authority that the Scripture says is due. Since "we have always taught that as long as the gospel does not go contrary to secular law one is to let secular law be effective, valid, and competent in those matters which it is able to handle, we therefore are unable to oppose anyone with arguments taken from Scripture, if in this instance it is necessary to fight back, even if the emperor himself attacks us, or whoever else may do so in his name."[32]

Brunner's first treatment of the problem of resistance follows this Protestant understanding closely. As a Reformed theologian, he cannot ignore the Calvinist tradition of resistance to tyranny, but he treats it primarily as a matter of historical interest. The idea of a right to resist an evil ruler provided a foundation for the modern idea of popular sovereignty, the idea that the people are the original source of all authority.[33] Political life today must be lived with a sense of general public responsibility for the affairs of state. "We no longer live at a time when one could trustfully leave the Elector or the 'strict and watchful lord' of Zürich, or the Council of Geneva, to do as they liked in everything that concerned the state . . . For good or for evil: today we are all responsible."[34]

This is in part at least the heritage of the reformers' search for legal limits on the power of hostile princes. Their cautious authorization of armed resistance is important because it helped to prepare the way for modern constitutional democracy. With respect to the state today, however, the operative rule is the biblical injunction to obedience. As for resistance, "only unavoidable necessity will avail to protect this dangerous action from the reproach of rebellion against God."[35] Perhaps this solution was initially satisfactory. It gave historical support to Europe's beleaguered democracies, while it suited Brunner's own reluctance to transpose demands for economic reforms into a call for socialist revolution. By 1943, however, the case was altered. The rise of the Nazi state threatened to destroy the church and the other orders of creation as well, and the havoc wrought by Hitler prompted Brunner to rethink the claim that armed resistance to tyrants cannot be justified ethically.

The key to the stress on obedience within the order of creation was not the idea that secular rulers are unusually wise or righteous. The point was that even a corrupt and impious regime serves some of God's purposes by maintaining the rudiments of public order in which the other orders of creation can continue to function. Moreover, because we cannot expect to understand the command of God apart from an understanding of the orders, the existing state, however bad it may be, remains the only effective school of politics. Reason's theoretical constructions cannot be put into practice consistently, for they always express our human aspirations in a one-sided way that leaves them only partly connected to reality. In the meantime, even tyrannical governments leave some avenues of protest and reform open to their people, if only to siphon off hostility and preserve their own power. To say that revolt against such a regime cannot be justified means we may not sacrifice the framework of order that does exist and the limited improvements that might be possible for a merely theoretical order which we cannot claim to know with any certainty.

The modern totalitarianism, however, represents a new problem. Hitler's Reich demanded, not only authority to govern, but the power to direct all other aspects of life as well. The independence of the church, the nurturing role of the family, and the cultural task of the school were swallowed up in the great political effort to achieve world domination for Germany.

Such a state, Brunner realized, does not maintain a framework for the other orders of creation. It destroys them in order to insure its own success, and it leaves very little hope for reform and moderation in its policies. Indeed, it controls the channels of political information as effectively as it restrains all forms of political action, so that a critical understanding of the order of government cannot even begin. "A political system so minutely organized and so rigidly centralized can leave no room for a right to resist based on positive law. . . . On the contrary, by their lawlessness, they destroy all law, and by their very existence outrage all sense of law."[36]

The problem is that the orders of creation doctrine, taken by itself, gives us no way to distinguish the genuine "sense of law" which is outraged by lawless dictatorships from a sentimental naiveté which tries to translate personal morality directly into political action. In all cases, we are told, the promptings of conscience and loving relationships to others must be expressed in forms that fit the requirements of the orders.[37] To do otherwise, we are told, would "ruin, destroy the world of institutions."[38]

In almost all cases, the warning is well taken, but the problem of totalitarianism points out a way in which the caution is overstated. The doctrine of the orders, by insisting that we can only know the command of God through our experience of the orders, assures that, once a state successfully controls the means of communication and education, there can be no moral objection to the order of the state as it is. If the state is the sole source of important information about public life, the only ground we have for complaints is our own unreliable conscience, our vague sense that something is amiss. These personal, idealistic, and ultimately one-sided visions, we have been repeatedly told, are not to be trusted as final guides to action. So when we want to know what to do, we must either assent to what the state tells us and do what it requires, or we must admit that we know nothing at all about the order of government and cannot rationally decide upon a course of action. This implication, which follows from strict adherence to the system in *The Divine Imperative,* is obviously not acceptable. So Brunner, in *Justice and the Social Order,* conceded that there is one point "of momentous importance" at which the natural law must be allowed to control our judgments and guide our actions.[39] Where a totalitarian government exceeds all limits and threatens to impose its own ideas of order, not only on the state, but on all the other orders as well, then we may appeal to a natural law understanding of the purposes of government. We may judge conclusively that this state is in disarray however firmly its power may be established in day-to-day terms of political stability or popular support. Then at least, reason's awareness that things might be other than they are and are not necessarily as we have been told is not just an idealistic vision. It is genuine moral knowledge. "Hence whenever people are suffering under the rigours of dictatorship, it is on the law of nature and the rights of man that they have set their hopes."[40]

Brunner's readiness to accept an opposition to totalitarianism based on natural law is more than a minor adjustment in his treatment of the orders of creation. If God's will is to be known in the order of the world, we need more than just the technical reason that lets us understand the material and social conditions that make our systems work. We need more, too, than the visionary reason that constructs theories and lets us see the world as it might be rather than strictly as it is. We need something much more like the practical reason of Aristotle and Aquinas, reason which understands the world as it is but also sees things in terms of the purposes they serve in bringing human beings to the full realization of their intellectual, social, and spiritual powers. If God's will is to be known in order, we must have this critical capacity to judge not merely whether an order is working but whether it is working *well*. Do the forms of law, of family, of work, and of worship that we have meet people's needs in ways that lead to a life closer to the human ideal? Almost any sort of order will allow us to survive; a good order helps us to flourish. If we fail to make that distinction, we lose our capacity to criticize a dicatorship that keeps the trains running on time, and in that way we limit the command of God by the power of a totalitarian state. A weak and ineffective government can always be criticized on the basis of what order requires, but a powerful dictatorship controls all those historical and social conditions within which, Brunner tells us, the commandment must be heard. Without critical, practical reason that evaluates order in terms of the purposes it serves, the order establishes its own authority just because it works. The divine imperative plays into the hands of those who already think themselves too close to gods.

The natural law case against totalitarianism in *Justice and the Social*

Order thus has wider implications for understanding ethics. It clears up some of the ambiguity which Brunner built into the concept of *Wortmächtigkeit* (capacity for speech) in the earlier debate with Karl Barth. *Wortmächtigkeit* is far more than the capacity to hear a word addressed to us by God as Brunner sometimes disarmingly suggested. Insofar as the Word of God is heard within the orders, the capacity for hearing the Word must include a knowledge of the human good and of the conditions for its achievement. Otherwise we would be unable to distinguish the Word of God from the human voice of the one who happens to be in charge of the order at that moment. *Wortmächtigkeit* now appears very much like the *ratio* (reason) of the Thomists.

This interpretation moves the doctrine of the orders of creation much close to traditional Catholic theories of natural law. It is doubtful that Brunner fully appreciated the significance of his natural law case against totalitarianism, and he certainly wanted to insist on the historic difference between Protestants and Catholics over the effect of sin on human reason.

> The Reformers lay far more stress than the mediaeval and Catholic teachers on the fact that sin obscures the capacity of human reason even in spheres which are accessible to rational knowledge. . . . Although they believed that the orders of creation are not hidden even from those who do not know the Creator and His creative will, they argued that secure and clear knowledge of the principles of mundane justice can only be obtained from the knowledge of the Creator and His creative will as it is revealed to us in Scriptural history and doctrine.[41]

Brunner states the Protestant tradition aptly, but the difference with Catholicism is not as sharp as he makes it seem. Indeed, Aquinas himself acknowledges that when we consider the difficulty of some moral reasoning and the probabilities of human error and evil creeping into our conclusions, we must recognize the importance of Scripture and the teaching of the church as a guide to a more secure hold on correct moral reasoning.[42] When we give proper attention to such reservations, the distance between Brunner's Protestant ethics and a Catholic account of moral reasoning is greatly narrowed.

That is not to say that the two positions become identical. Especially, Brunner would differ with the Thomists over the extension of reason's powers from the moral into the theological realm. While the distinction between revealed and natural knowledge has always been important in Catholic thought, the scope of natural knowledge has usually included a "natural theology," a minimal knowledge of God as the all-powerful source of human life and worthy object of human worship. Such natural theology does not rely on the Christian revelation in Scripture or tradition but is confined to what can be known about God by reason alone. Catholic thinkers treat this natural theology in close connection with the natural law knowledge of morality, and the papal pronouncements that led to the modern revival of Thomist ethics often touch on natural law morality only as a branch of natural theology.[43] For Brunner, as for Barth and others who deny the *analogia entis,* the distinction between natural law and natural theology must be more sharp. The reasoned knowledge of human life may take us a good distance beyond what is required for mere survival, but it cannot for these Protestants lift us out of the human realm altogether. It cannot tell us anything about God.

Consensus on the theological foundations of ethics remains elusive, then, but we should not underestimate the importance of the convergence between Brunner's orders of creation and Catholic natural law theory. On matters of practical human choice, a large measure of agreement on the terms of the discussion has been reached. The orders of creation, no less than the natural law, are fully known only as they are evaluated in connection with human purposes and understood as conditions for the best possible human life. It would be simplistic to expect that basic statement of terms to resolve all the substantive questions about what constitutes a good life, but neither should we underrate the importance of the agreement. When the problems of ethics are seen chiefly as problems of preservation, the conflict between sinful individuals and their unruly desires is inevitably the order of the day, and discussions in ethics will turn principally on how this conflict can be regulated within survivable limits. Discussion cannot even begin, then, with those who claim that more is possible and who want to talk about institutions and order in terms of human purposes. Brunner's doctrine of the orders in its later expressions makes discussion possible on those terms for Protestants as it has been for Catholic natural law theorists since Thomas. At the same time, precisely because the moral discussion is centered on human purposes and does not presuppose theological commitments, it is open in principle to all persons who care to formulate an idea of the good life that is consistent with the powers and limitations of human beings generally.

In *Justice and the Social Order,* Brunner's theory thus achieves the openness to general understanding and participation that he sought in his initial formulation of the orders of creation and in his polemic exchange with Karl Barth. The natural law which stands as a controlling idea and final point of appeal against the present workings of the orders assures that the choices Christians make can also be understood by and explained to others.

For Barth, of course, these terms are impossible. The appeal to natural law which Brunner makes into the last defense against totalitarianism remains for Barth an idolatrous confusion of human will with divine command. The question then arises, How would Barth's ethic of the Word of God respond to the totalitarian challenge?

NOTES

1. Alec R. Vidler and W. A. Whitehouse, *Natural Law: A Christian Reconsideration* (London: SCM Press, 1946).

2. For a major portion of Aquinas's writing on natural law, see Dino Bigongiari, ed., *The Political Ideas of St. Thomas Aquinas* (New York: Hafner Press, 1953), 3–64. An important modern treatment of natural law is Josef Fuchs, *Natural Law* (New York: Sheed and Ward, 1965). A good introduction to the subject is found in Timothy O'Connell, *Principles for a Catholic Morality* (New York: Seabury Press, 1978), 117–95.

3. Rom. 2:14.

4. Bigongiari, ed., *Political Ideas of Aquinas,* 32.

5. For a brief history of these developments in moral theology, see Bernard Häring, *Free and Faithful in Christ* (New York: Seabury Press, 1978), 1: 45–54.

6. Scheler's major work was *Formalism in Ethics and a Nonformal Ethics of Values.*

7. Dietrich von Hildebrand, *Ethics* (Chicago: Franciscan Herald Press, 1952).

8. O'Connell, *Principles,* 117–24.

9. Jacques Maritain, *Integral Humanism,* trans. Joseph W. Evans (New York: Charles Scribner's Sons, 1968).

10. Heinrich Rommen, *The Natural Law,* trans. Thomas R. Hanley (St. Louis: B. Herder, 1948).

11. See chapter 3, 65–66.

12. Brunner, *Divine Imperative,* 485–86.

13. Ibid.; see also Reinhold Niebuhr, *The Nature and Destiny of Man* (New York: Charles Scribner's Sons, 1949), 1:150–77.

14. Brunner, *Divine Imperative,* 484.

15. "Rerum novarum," in *Seven Great Encyclicals,* ed. William J. Gibbons (New York: Paulist Press, 1963), 4.

16. Brunner, *Divine Imperative,* 484.

17. Ibid., 96.

18. Aristotle, *Nicomachean Ethics,* trans. Martin Ostwald (Indianapolis: Bobbs-Merrill, 1962), 5.

19. Brunner, *Divine Imperative,* 645.

20. Ibid.

21. Nathaniel Micklem, *National Socialism and Christianity*, Oxford Pamphlets on World Affairs, no. 18 (Oxford: At the Clarendon Press, 1939).

22. See Alan Donagan, *The Theory of Morality* (Chicago: University of Chicago Press, 1979), 15–17.

23. Thomas Aquinas, *Truth*, trans. James V. McGlynn (Chicago: Henry Regnery Company, 1953), 2: 337.

24. Brunner, *Justice*, 95.

25. *St. Augustine on Free Will*, trans. Carroll Mason Sparrow, University of Virginia Studies, no. 4 (Charlottesville, Va.: University of Virginia Press, 1947), 11–13. See also Bigongiari, ed., *Political Ideas of Anquinas*, 72.

26. Victor Cathrein, *Moralphilosophie* (Freiburg i. B.: Herder'sche Verlagshandlung, 1893), 2: 602–5. Brunner was thoroughly familiar with this widely used textbook of Roman Catholic ethics.

27. Brunner, *Justice*, 93.

28. Quentin Skinner, *The Foundations of Modern Political Thought* (Cambridge: At the University Press, 1978), II: 191–206.

29. *Luther's Works: Letters II*, ed. Gottfried Krodel (Philadelphia: Fortress Press, 1972), 49: 432–33.

30. John Calvin, *Institutes*, 2: 1519.

31. See especially the Protestant political treatises in Julian H. Franklin, ed., *Constitutionalism and Resistance in the Sixteenth Century* (Indianapolis: Bobbs-Merrill, 1969).

32. *Luther's Works*, 49: 432.

33. Brunner, *Divine Imperative*, 693.

34. Ibid., 462.

35. Ibid., 474.

36. Brunner, *Justice*, 95.

37. Idem, *Divine Imperative*, 645.

38. Idem, *Justice*, 128–29.

39. Ibid., 93.

40. Ibid., 95.

41. Ibid., 91–92.

42. Bigongiari, ed., *Political Ideas of Aquinas*, 17.

43. Fuchs, *Natural Law*, 147–50.

5
A CHURCH FOR
DANGEROUS TIMES

When Adolf Hitler became chancellor of Germany on January 20, 1933, the situation of the German churches was dramatically different from the time at the close of World War I which inspired Barth's *Epistle to the Romans*. In place of the confusion which marked the collapse of imperial Germany, there was now a strident certainty on all sides, from the opposition of the socialists and communists—who were soon to be persecuted out of existence—to the enthusiasm of the German Christian Faith Movement, organized in 1931 to carry Nazi principles into the Protestant churches. Above all, there was now a single center of initiative, one place where action began and one power to which the churches had to respond. Within months, Hitler's efforts to reorganize all important institutions under state supervision and to exclude "non-Aryans" from leadership positions caused a crisis in the churches, especially where members and pastors of Jewish descent were concerned.

No one can say that the Christians of Germany were always wise in evaluating these events or effective in responding to them. There was the substantial German Christian movement, which identified Hitler's triumph with the Christian hope, and there was an even larger number who accepted the new regime as the best chance for restoring their country's pride and their own prosperity but who thought little about how these aims fit with their Christian faith. Many Christians in Gemany welcomed the new order or accepted it as inevitable as most Christians in most places have responded to political changes throughout history. Christian support for the Nazi regime is embarrassing in retrospect, but it should not be surprising.

What is remarkable is that there were those who did not acquiesce. Some, like the Bonhoeffer family, feared and despised Hitler from the outset. Others welcomed the new national leadership but refused to confuse political and diplomatic goals with the mission of the church. Together, these persons not only made their arguments against the Nazification of the churches; they actually maintained an alternative structure to oversee the congregations, choose the leadership, and provide for the pastors. When the universities, the press, and the labor unions all conformed to the National Socialist *Gleichschaltung*,[1] the Confessing Church[2] resisted. Though it included only a minority of German Protestants, though it suffered from internal disunity, and though it was ultimately overwhelmed by events, it firmly maintained that "Jesus Christ, as he is witnessed to us in Holy Scripture, is the one Word of God to whom we must listen, whom we must trust and obey in life and in death."[3] Few in Germany at the time could understand this insistence on a center of loyalty and value utterly separate from the state. The story of how some Christians were able to maintain that faith and organize themselves to sustain it is one of the most important stories of the church of this or any century.

It is also an answer to a question we have asked repeatedly in these pages: "How can obedience to the Word of God become a public choice, an act that engages the understanding and affects the choices of others?" For the Confessing Church, the answer was that obedience to the Word of God becomes public in the church. God's will is known and made known, not in the lives of solitary individuals, but in their common life in the church. It is no accident that this answer is also Karl Barth's answer. The theologian of the Word of God answered criticism of his ethics at least in part by what he did to help organize the Confessing Church and to draft its statement of faith. Having turned to Brunner and the Roman Catholic moral theologians to see how the Word of God might be known through the natural law or the orders of creation, we now return to Barth, who insisted that the Word is known in the context of the church.

Barth's emphasis on the church as the place where the Word is heard reflects the development of his thought during the 1920s. From his singular emphasis on God's Word addressed to the crisis in human society, Barth turned to the trinitarian formulations of the *analogia fidei*: God speaks to us as creator, redeemer, and reconciler. The one Word conveys three messages. Finally, as Barth began to write his systematic theology, he realized that a full account must also include attention to where and how the threefold Word is heard. God addresses individual persons, to be sure, but *as part of a people*. The story of faith is not a series of stories about isolated individuals. It is the account of a community whom God summons to a continuing covenant partnership. Only when we understand that about the hearers of God's Word do we fully understand the Word itself.

After 1927 Barth scrapped his plan to write a lengthy work on "Christian dogmatics" and started instead on the volumes that would occupy him for the rest of his life, the *Church Dogmatics*.[4] The change in name is significant. Henceforward, the faith of the individual Christian in Barth's thought finds its proper place in the faith of the church.

This important change affected Barth's ethics as well. In the *Church Dogmatics* there is less attention to the "child of God who knows his father's will"[5] and more to the church as a community of attention and obedience to the Word of God. Increasingly, what was said of the individual believer in *The Epistle to the Romans* is now understood in the context of the church. The church is the true object of the command of God and the true locus of obedience. Barth retracts none of what he has already said, but he asks us to read it in a somewhat different way. We must not think of the obedience of a solitary individual addressed by a Word out of all connection with everything previously known; rather we think of persons in a community which has a history of obedience. This community of obedience is the church, but it is quite unlike the church described by Brunner, which takes its place among the orders of creation, performing special functions of worship, proclamation, and intercession that nicely complement the distinctive tasks of the other orders. Barth's obedient community responds to a single source of authority, God's command in the Scriptures, and it refuses to confuse that authority with any other power or take its cues for behavior from the social requirements of any other system. Far from adjusting its own life in response to God's commandment as known in the other orders of creation, Barth's church insists on the freedom to order its life in response to God's command in Scripture alone. It calls on all persons and especially all rulers, whether or not they share the faith of the church, to understand the independent authority to which the church responds and to refrain from any acts that might restrict this freedom. Against every power that thinks it can define a human good and organize society to pursue it, the church claims the freedom to stand outside that project and to live by its own obedience.

The "German Christians"

The test of this claim was not long in coming. Hitler moved at once to reassure the religious leaders of his support for what he called "positive Christianity," but he made it clear that he also expected their cooperation in his restructuring of German life and institutions. A commission was appointed to effect the union of the various Protestant territorial churches (*Landeskirchen*) into a single national church, restrictions were placed on church schools and organizations, and, ominously, calls were heard for enforcing the "Aryan clause" in the churches. This would exclude persons of Jewish descent from holding office or membership in the national church.

For Catholics, relations to the new German state were eased by the Vatican's status as a separate sovereign power. This allowed the German bishops to arrange a church-state treaty, or concordat, between the papacy and the German government. Such agreements had been used since Napoleonic times to stabilize relationships between the Roman Catholic Church and powerful new European states. The concordat negotiated with Hitler's government in 1933 provided considerable independence for Catholic schools and organizations, and it allowed the clergy to go about their pastoral duties without pressure for political conformity. At the same time, the Nazi regime no doubt gained support from German Catholics and some international standing from the recognition implied in the treaty. Later writers have criticized the Vatican's cooperation with the Hitler regime, and it seems that the Nazi policy makers were, indeed, more aware than their ecclesiastical counterparts of the propaganda value of the concordat. Nevertheless, the agreement of 1933 secured for the Catholic Church precisely the freedom of action that Protestants in the Confessing Church were seeking at about the same time.[6]

The Protestant situation, with its historic union of throne and altar, was more complicated. While the total number of Protestants in Germany was slightly larger than the number of Catholics, the Protestant churches had been divided ever since the Reformation, not only along confessional lines, but also according to German political divisions. Thus, the Lutheran Church in Hanover, for example, was distinct not only from the Reformed Church in Hanover but from the Lutheran Church in neighboring Bremen. The political union of the German territories under Prussian rule in the nineteenth century did not end these ecclesiastical divisions, so that in 1933 most of Germany's Protestants were organized into territorial churches. Some of these were Lutheran, some Reformed, and some were Union churches which combined the two groups. In addition to these state-supported churches, there were a small number of Protestants in groups such as Baptists, Jehovah's Witnesses, or independent Lutherans. These "free churches" were organized without the support of the government.

On July 23, 1933, special elections were held to choose new leadership for all of the territorial churches. The German Christians, supported by the Nazi propaganda apparatus, won overwhelmingly. The administrative structures of most of the territorial churches were henceforth controlled by leaders committed to the formation of a unified national Protestant church in accord with National Socialist principles. Pressure from the state to conform to the new order was now matched by a powerful force within the church which was prepared to deny its own freedom and commit the church totally to service of the German national ideal. The imperatives for Christians would henceforth be drawn from the secular struggle to reshape German life along the lines described in the Nazi platform.

Those who opposed this Nazification of German Protestantism were now confronted with stark options. They could, as an act of protest, quit their territorial church and join a free church. They might even try to form their own free church if they could gather sufficient support. In either case, they would be surrendering the state-supported church to the German Christians. They would be making an act of protest, but they would also be acknowledging by their withdrawal that the church they were leaving legitimately belonged to the German Christian majority.

Another, stronger position would be to declare that for theological reasons the church cannot put itself at the service of the state's program. The church is bound by its historic confessions of faith to insist upon its own freedom, and when it no longer makes that demand, it ceases to be the church. No majority vote or administrative action can change this requirement, and the church leadership which surrenders this freedom forfeits its office in the act. True church authority remains with those who are faithful to the historic confessions. Which party the state supports and who ends up in control of the administrative machinery are irrelevant.

It is important to see the sharp difference between the free church idea and this second strategy, which provided the foundation for the Confessing Church. Those who took leadership in the Confessing Church did not conceive that they were forming a new religious organization, a "denomination" in the American sense. The Confessing Church claimed to be *the* Protestant church, set against a Reich church government which had the support of the state but which had no real right to define the terms of church life against those who were loyal to the Reformation confessions. The demand of the Confessing Church was not for a separation out of the faithful but for a declaration of the mind of the church. What the confessional leadership wanted was a *synod* (from the Greek *synodos,* literally a "meeting of paths"), an assembly that would rule decisively on what the church had to be and to believe.

The Barmen Synod

This Synod convened on May 29, 1934, in the Gemarke Church in Barmen, a community within the city of Wuppertal, which is located in the industrial northwest of Germany. A total of 138 members, representing the confessional parties in eighteen territorial churches, met for three days to settle organizational matters and to adopt a theological declaration for the Confessing Chruch.[7]

The theological document issued at the close of the Synod was largely the work of Karl Barth. He has given his own humorous account of how his Reformed theology prevailed over that of his Lutheran co-workers when they met to draft a preliminary declaration. "The Lutheran Church slept and the Reformed Church kept awake," says Barth. During a three-hour break after lunch, "I revised the text of the six statements, fortified by strong coffee and one or two Brazilian cigars. . . . The result was that by that evening there was a text. I don't want to boast, but it was really my text."[8] The preliminary text was subjected to thorough study and some revisions during the Synod, but the final declaration is recognizably the one that the wakeful Barth drafted on May 16.

Barth's task was more difficult than he makes it sound. Though there was wide agreement that the new German Christian church government had violated the confessions of faith of the historic Protestant churches, this renewed attention to the confessions in itself compounded the problems of drawing up a statement that could satisfy both Lutheran and Reformed traditions. The German Christians' indifference to theology made their Confessing Church opponents more attentive to it, but that, in turn, made them aware of old differences that had been largely ignored during the era of liberal theology.

Barth's solution was characteristic of his method. He insisted that a declaration of faith must not be a general statement of theological truths for all time to come but a faithful account of what the Word of God has to say to the church today.[9] He did not seek to resolve the differences between Lutheran and Reformed positions because the task was rather to articulate that on which both confessions were agreed: The German Christian movement marked a defection from the faith and a danger to the church.

The Barmen Declaration

The Synod's document, then, was to be a "declaration," not a "confession." It is not a final statement of doctrinal truth. The drafting committee proposed six articles, each consisting of a scriptural text, an interpretation, and a rejection.[10] The interpretation, as Hans Asmussen said in presenting the document to the Synod, states how the church must read the text in the context of its crisis: "For the present time we have been given this understanding of the Biblical text."[11] The rejection then specifies what the church must reject on the basis of the text and its interpretation.

As an address to the situation of the German churches, the Barmen Declaration speaks for itself as the Synod intended. It is, however, worth considering the broader implications of this document, at least as they were present for Barth when he wrote it. The Barmen Synod preceded by only a few months the writing of "No!", his intense attack on Brunner's natural theology. Barth's comments on the Barmen Declaration make it clear that he meant it to reject more than the rejections explicitly stated.[12]

For Barth, the excesses of the German Christians merely made evident the flaws in a theology that had sometimes escaped criticism when it had served more acceptable purposes. What is wrong with the theology of the German Christians is not only that it is National Socialist. What is wrong fundamentally is that it is a "natural" theology. It seeks a source of understanding and direction for Christian life in some order outside of the Word of God as it is heard in the church through the Scriptures. The German Christians search for directions in the narrow ambitions of German nationalism, and that is deplorable, but a better source of inspiration—say, the orders of creation delineated by Brunner—would not in Barth's view improve the underlying theology. Hence the first article of the Barmen Declaration is implicitly a rejection of all sources for the teaching of the church which might be shared with those outside the community of revelation.

1. "I am the way, the truth, and the life; no one comes to the Father except by me" (John 14:6). "Truly, truly, I say to you, whoever does not enter the sheepfold by the gate, but goes in by another way, is a thief and a murderer. I am the door; if anyone enters through me, he shall be blessed" (John 10:1, 9).

Jesus Christ, as he is witnessed to us in Holy Scripture, is the one Word of God to whom we must listen, whom we must trust and obey in life and in death.

> We reject the false teaching that the church could and must recognize as a source of its proclamation in addition to and beside this one Word of God, other events and powers, concepts and truths as God's revelation.

Thus, the first article of the Barmen Declaration is a statement of what Bonhoeffer would call "theological positivism."[13] If the German Christians have joined faith and patriotism in an unacceptable combination, that is a warning of the consequences whenever the Word of God is subjected to criticism or corroboration from some other source. Neither reason, nor history, nor the orders of creation have any authority against the words that become the Word in Scripture.

This insistence on a single source of authoritative teaching in the church has implications both for those who tie the church too closely to political movements and for those who separate them too radically. Obviously, the German Christians who claimed that the "law of the German people is the law of God" and demanded the Nazification of the church along with the rest of society stand condemned by the rejections of Barmen. Barth, however, intended that the second article and its rejections should also reach those Christians who were less enthusiastic for Hitler's cause but who believed that the church should stay out of politics and let the business of government proceed according to its own rules.

> 2. "Jesus Christ is made by God to be our wisdom and righteousness, our sanctification and redemption" (1 Cor. 1:30).
>
> As Jesus Christ is God's pledge (*Zuspruch*) for the forgiveness of all our sins, so with equal seriousness is he God's powerful claim (*Anspruch*) over our whole life. Through him we receive a joyous release from all the godless bonds of this world for free and thankful service to his creatures.
>
> We reject the false teaching that there could be areas of our life in which we belong, not to Jesus Christ, but to other lords, areas in which we do not need his justification and sanctification.

From Luther's time forward, Protestantism has tended to draw sharp distinctions between gospel and law, Christian community and civil community, or church and state. Where Catholic moral theology ranks secular and spiritual purposes in hierarchical order, insisting that spiritual tasks complete but do not compete with secular ones, Protestants tend to set the worldly and the religious spheres alongside one another and so, subtly, to set them in opposition.[14] The world of unredeemed sinners requires a harsh justice that would be inappropriate in the community of Christians, while the Christians observe a trust and forbearance among themselves that would quickly lead to chaos if they tried to run the world that way.[15] Brunner's idea of the orders of creation as relatively autonomous structures, governed each by its own set of material and social imperatives, is simply the latest development of this Protestant way of thinking. It begins by realistically assessing the way the world works, but Barth saw that it could end too often with Christians refusing the difficult task of living their faith in the world and settling instead for a comfortable accommodation with the powers that be. In the face of the grave danger posed by the German Christians, those who confess the Reformation faith must now go beyond the reformers' politics.

> The formulae of the Reformation era are notably no longer sufficient here. Today, indeed, the devil hides himself behind them. To be faithful to the way of the Reformation, we must return to the Scripture itself and set this forth as certain and valid: Jesus Christ the Lord cares for all our needs, but also claims our whole existence—he is high priest, but also king, just as he alone is also prophet.[16]

The third and fourth articles of the Barmen Declaration concern the internal order of the church and its relation to ideas, goals, and movements outside of itself. Implicit in both is the "Jewish question" and the demand of the German Christians that the church reorganize itself to exclude those of "non-Aryan" descent from its offices and membership just as the universities and the civil service were doing at the time.

It may seem strange, initially, that the "Jewish question" should become an internal issue for the Christian churches, but we must remember that for the Nazis the Jews were a race, not a religious community. Consequently, Christians who had even one Jewish parent or grandparent found themselves in danger of exclusion from their churches and, if they were pastors, from their pulpits. There is no way to know how many pastors and church members found themselves in this situation, but the number was not small, and it was in relation to this question of its own order and standards that the church first was forced to deal with the Nazi anti-Semitism that it had largely ignored.

3. "But let us be righteous in love and grow in all things toward Christ, who is the head, in whom the whole body is knit together" (Eph. 4:15–16).

The Christian Church is the company of brethren in which Jesus Christ is now present as Lord by the Holy Spirit in Word and Sacrament. It has to bear witness with its faith and with its obedience, with its message and with its order, in the midst of the world of sin as a church of sinners saved by grace, that it is his property alone, that it lives and wants to live only by his care and his instruction, awaiting his appearance.

We reject the false teaching that the church might alter the character of its message and its order to suit its own pleasure or changes in the prevailing philosophy or politics.

The third article of the Declaration identifies the church as a "company of brethren in which Jesus Christ is now present as Lord by the Holy Spirit in Word and Sacrament." Any thought of other criteria for membership is implicitly ruled out, and the rejection pointedly insists that the order of the church may not be changed to suit prevailing ideas in the culture.

The fourth article, similarly, insists that ministry in the church is an office of service that grows out of the life of the whole community. Ministers must not be confused with authority figures in the society, nor can the society's grounds for choosing or excluding persons as teachers, officials, jurists, and the like be applied to the office of the pastor.

4. "You know that worldly princes rule and authorities have power. But it shall not be so among you. Anyone who wants to be your ruler must be your servant" (Matt. 20:25–26).

The various offices of the church empower no lordship of one over another, but the exercise of the ministry pledged and commended to the whole congregation.

We reject the false teaching that the church could set up for itself or allow itself to be given special leaders with authority apart from this ministry.

On these issues, then, the Confessing Church's resistance to the application of the "Aryan clause" and the expulsion of Jewish Christians was based. The issue was narrowly drawn on the question of the freedom and internal order of the church, and the broader issue of the civil and human rights of Jews who are not Christians was not raised. Nor could it have been, for the Confessing Church as a body was not united in its attitude toward the "Jewish question" or toward any other matters of Nazi policy save the issue of the freedom of the church. Much later, Barth expressed regret that he had not been more explicit in his attack on the Nazis racial policies. "Of course, in 1934 no text in which I had done that would have been acceptable even to the Confessing Church, given the atmosphere that there was then. But that does not excuse me for not having at least gone through the motions of fighting."[17]

The fifth article deals explicitly with church-state relations. Here Barth has devised a masterful compromise between his own conviction

110

that the Reformation teaching which divides the church sharply from the world is obsolete and the more conservative attitude of the Synod as a whole. The urgent task of the Barmen Synod was to warn against the Nazi state's drive to control and order all of life. On that point the delegates at Barmen could most probably agree, particularly when it was expressed in the language of Augustine and Luther, who saw the state as a necessary device for the punishment and restraint of evil in a sinful world.

> 5. "Fear God; honor the King" (1 Pet. 2:17). Scripture tells us that *the state* has by divine appointment, in this not yet redeemed world in which the church also stands, the task to work for justice and peace according to the measure of human insight and capacity, by punishment and exercise of restraint. The church acknowledges in gratitude and honor to God the goodness of this appointment. It remembers God's kingdom, God's commandment and righteousness, and with these, the responsibility of the rulers and the ruled. It trusts and obeys the power of the Word, through which God upholds all things.
>
> We reject the false teaching that the state could and should, beyond its specific function, become the sole and total order of human life and so fulfill also the role of the church. We reject the false teaching that the church could and should beyond its specific function take on the style, duties, and honors of a state and thus itself become an organ of the state.

Barth's theological concern was to reformulate the traditional view of the state in a way which did not leave an opening to construe its functions along the lines of natural law or the orders of creation. The state is a divine "appointment" (*Anordnung*), not an "order" (*Ordnung*) of creation. The pointed choice not to use the familiar word favored by Brunner and by some of the German Christian theologians marks Barth's determination that upholding the indispensable role of the state in maintaining justice and order should not become an excuse for inventing independent claims to know what the state's order requires. The German Christians claimed to know from the imperatives of history that Adolf Hitler was empowered to begin a new era for the German people so that the changes he made in the role of the state were valid. Barth wants not so much to dispute that claim as to show that the whole way of argument on which it is based is wrong. It is from Scripture, and not from reason or history, that we learn the function of the state. The rejection of totalitarianism which concludes the fifth article does not rest on a better understanding of the state but on an understanding of the commandments of God. Thus Barth preserves the reformers' teaching on the distinctive functions of church and state, while he neatly subordinates the distinction to the primary fact that all such differentiations depend immediately on the will of God.

The sixth article concludes the Declaration with a forceful statement of the freedom of the church. As the church must be free to perform its own special function, so it cannot be required to put itself at the service of any other program. Among other things, this implies that the church of the Reformation is not available to carry out a political program of racial "purification."

> 6. "Behold, I am with you always, even to the end of the world" (Matt. 28:20). "God's word is not bound" (2 Timothy 2:9).
>
> *The appointed task of the church,* in which its freedom is founded, consists in teaching in the place of Christ, and so in the service of his own word and work, through preaching and sacrament, the message of the free grace of God to all people.
>
> We reject the false teaching that the church in human self-glorification might put the word and work of the Lord in the service of any arbitrarily chosen wishes, purposes, and plans.
>
> The Confessional Synod of the German Evangelical Church declares that it sees the inescapable theological foundation of the German Evangelical Church as a federation of Confessing Churches in the recognition of these truths and the rejection of these errors. It encourages all who can join in this declaration to be mindful of these theological principles in their decisions in church politics. It asks all concerned to return to the unity of faith, love, and hope.
>
> *Verbum Dei manet in aeternum.*

The Word of God
and the Freedom of the Church

It is at Barmen, then, that we see at last a working version of the ethic of the Word of God. Attentiveness to Scripture cuts across the uncertainty that marks the human situation and provides a clear word to guide the Christian's response for the present time. The competing claims in the world, based on history, politics, and power, offer no direction; and the Christian responses based on reason, nature, or a reading of the orders of creation provide nothing better. The only way beyond the confusion is a single-minded reliance on the Word, which comes, however, not to the individual Christian in isolation, but to the church assembled together. Among the delegates at Barmen there were differing attitudes toward the Hitler regime, and when they dispersed to their work across Germany, there would be bitter disagreements over precisely what the freedom they had declared at the Synod required. Nevertheless, there was at Barmen a moment of moral certainty which was adequate, not to all times and places, but to the needs of that time. Barth had insisted since *The Epistle to the Romans* that Christian ethics is made up of such moments of attention when the commandment of God becomes clear in experience.

It is appropriate to the act-deontology of Barth's ethics that the Barmen Declaration leaves the question of future relationships between church and state unsettled. Barth himself was convinced that the opposition between the churches and the Nazi regime must intensify if the Synod took its declaration seriously. He was caught in such a conflict himself later in 1934, when he refused to take a new loyalty oath imposed on university teachers and other civil servants and so lost his position at the University of Bonn. Shortly thereafter he left Germany and returned to live in Switzerland.

In the freedom of his new position as professor of theology at Basel, Barth was able to explain more fully the implications of the position he had drafted at Barmen. In 1938, he published an article on church and state[18] which attempted to set out their relationship on scriptural grounds, without recourse to the arguments from history and reason which, he believed, had flawed previous efforts. A study of Pilate's role in the execution of Jesus leads Barth to the question many were asking: What is the Christian response to an unjust state which no longer uses its power to punish and restrain for good purposes, but corrupts justice and begins to destroy the innocent?

Barth refuses to answer in general terms, as though there could be some universal duty of obedience or a right to resist a dictator that applies everywhere and provides a changeless answer to the question. Rather, Barth says that the state in the New Testament is treated as a "power" or "authority," one of the superhuman forces in the universe which are subordinated to Christ, or at least are in the process of being subordinated. "In him everything in heaven and on earth was created, not only things visible, but also the invisible orders of thrones, sovereignties, authorities, and powers: the whole universe has been created through him and for him."[19]

Significantly, the New Testament speaks of "powers" and "authorities" in the plural, not as though there were some one essential idea of the state or an abstract definition of its function. There is a plurality of powers, each with distinctive characteristics . . .

And all these entities which are so difficult to distinguish (probably they should all be included under the comprehensive heading *angeloi*) constitute created, but invisible, spiritual and heavenly powers, which exercise, in and above the rest of creation, a certain independence, and in this independence have a certain superior dignity, task, and function, and exert a certain real influence.[20]

Properly speaking, then, the Christian has to deal with *states,* not *the state.* The appropriate response is to confront a particular state as a given reality. The task is what the New Testament calls "discerning the spirits" to see which ones are of God, or more precisely, to see whether this power has recognized its proper subordination to Christ or exists for the time being in rebellious defiance. The specificity of this judgment precludes any general rules about resistance or obedience. Christians must take their directions from the reality they discern at the time. "Thus there is clearly no cause for the Church to act as though it lived, in relation to the State, in a night in which all cats are grey. It is much more a question of continual decisions and therefore of distinctions between one State and another, between the State of yesterday and the State of today."[21]

On this basis, Barth moves quite boldly toward an authorization of Christian opposition to the totalitarian order that had been firmly established in Germany and was threatening the rest of Europe. "When I consider the deepest and most central content of the New Testament exhortation," Barth wrote in 1938, "I should say that we are justified, from the point of view of exegesis, in regarding the 'democratic conception of the state' as a justifiable expansion of the thought of the New Testament."[22] Christians in democratic states must be prepared for military service, a point which Barth later reinforced by himself joining the Swiss militia. "We may have grave misgivings about the way in which the Swiss state seeks to be a just state, but all the same, we cannot maintain that it confronts the Church like 'the Beast out of the abyss' of Revelation 13. But this may and should be said of more than one other State today, against which it is worthwhile to defend our own legal administration."[23] After the outbreak of war in 1939, Barth wrote open letters of encouragement to Christians in France and England, urging them to stand firm in the sufferings of war and calling their cause a necessary action on behalf of civic peace and justice which God desires for the world.[24]

As for those Christians living in Germany, Barth seems to encourage them to resist their totalitarian state as he encouraged those in the democracies to support theirs. Christians, as Paul and the reformers taught, may be obliged to respect an unjust state, but this "can in no case mean that the Church and its members will approve, and wish of their own free will to further, the claims and undertakings of the State, if once the State power is turned not to the protection but to the suppression of the preaching of justification."[25] At the very least, Christians in an unjust state must withdraw from active support of the state's programs and imperialistic ambitions. Moreover, they must not conceal this withdrawal. They must express it openly in intercessory prayer for the state which has gone astray. Public intercession as a form of resistance would be, as Barth put it, "very calm and dignified,"[26] and far removed from a political conspiracy to overthrow the state.[27] Nevertheless, it would hardly be well received in a state like Hitler's Germany.

Is it perhaps the case, then, that the ethics which grows out of the Barmen Declaration commits the church to the service of the "democratic conception of the state" and sets it in inevitable opposition—however "calm and dignified"—to totalitarian forms of governmental power? That would be a strange reversal for a theologian who had insisted that God's Word cannot be captured in any human system, but many thought they saw that in Barth's support of the Allies after the outbreak of the Second World War. These readers were then startled, and indeed outraged, when after 1945 Barth refused to condemn Communist totalitarianism in the same terms he had used against the Nazis and suggested that the West and the Marxists might be equally far from the kingdom of God.[28]

Barth's position, condemning one totalitarianism in the strongest terms and treating another as no worse than its democratic rivals, is not inconsistent, but it is a reminder of the uniqueness of his ethical method. It is a risky business to conclude that a Barthian ethics must support democracy or condemn totalitarianism precisely because Barth refuses to make the sort of generalizations that would permit these conclusions.

The rather conservative cast of much Christian political thought begins with the distinction between the functions of the state and those of other elements of society. The state provides a framework of order within which the work of education, culture, worship, and economic production can go on. It is essential that the state be constrained within this limited role, but so long as it performs its own tasks and does not interfere with other social functions, it deserves the support and active participation of Christians as citizens. Totalitarianism appears in this perspective as an aberration, an exceptional case in which the state has overstepped its boundaries and must be forced back into its proper role so that the respect which it rightly deserves can once again be freely given.

A more radical political theology has developed in recent years to argue that all governments fail today to provide the framework of order that is the state's legitimate function.[29] Forms of economic exploitation which dominate both state and family preclude an appropriate ordering of society, while the distorted channels of public communication are used to deny the effects of the exploitation and thus to corrupt the institutions of education and culture. The aberrations of modern totalitarianism are not, according to the political theologians, an unusual failure of the state to function properly. Totalitarianism is merely an unpleasant instance of the general failure of the state to provide a framework of order for modern industrial society.

Both conservative and radical theologians, then, begin their reflections on politics with the function of the state. What the conservatives and the radicals have in common is a general idea of what the state ought to do that provides the basis for their particular judgments on particular states.

Barth knows this language about the state's proper function very well. "The task to work for justice and peace according to the measure of human insight and capacity, by punishment and exercise of restraint" appears in the Barmen Declaration along with similar phrases in Barth's other writings during this period. What distinguishes Barth is his refusal to turn this admittedly valid statement about the state's proper function into a general rule that would tell us how to act toward the state. Hence, Barth would probably oppose the radicalism of today's political theology with the same vehemence he directed against the conservatism of Brunner and the Catholic natural law theorists.

Those who use the description of the state's function as a general rule for action put themselves precisely where we found Brunner at the end of chapter 4. They have an idea of the human good that the state is supposed to serve which allows them to enter into a public discussion and evaluation of the performance of particular states. Christians can thus explain their own attitude toward state policies and encourage others to act with them on the basis of an idea of what the state is supposed to do that everyone else could also share. Like the Christian engineer who, Brunner says, builds sound bridges rather than Christian bridges, the Christian community would aim to create a good state together with its neighbors. The result need not be a "Christian" state, and the community which discusses and evaluates the state would be an inclusive one.

What Barth seeks, however, is, not a general community of discussion, but a particular community of discernment. The task imposed on

Christians is not to make a Christian state, but neither is it to make a good state.

> The tasks and problems which the Christian community is called to share, in fulfillment of its political responsibility, are "natural," secular, profane tasks and problems. But the norm by which it should be guided is anything but natural: it is the only norm which it can believe in and accept as a spiritual norm, and is derived from the clear law of its own faith, not from the obscure workings of a system outside itself: it is from knowledge of this norm that it will make its decisions in the political sphere.[30]

With respect to the state, a certain discernment of spirits is called for, a responsiveness to the Word of God which identifies this state or that one as subordinate or not yet subordinated to the power of God. That discernment helps the church to find a proper attitude toward the state, but even then the aim is not to reform the state but to help the church to go about its own task more effectively.

What the church demands from the state is its own freedom, not civic or political righteousness. Christians are not empowered to correct the errors and excesses of those in authority, but they must insist that, whatever the state does, the church remains free to carry out its ministry of prayer and proclamation, ordering its own life for the fulfillment of those tasks. The Synod of Barmen spelled out in some detail what this meant in relation to the Nazi state. The church cannot accept exclusions which are based on the state's own program of "racial purity." The church cannot exchange the biblical concept of leadership as service for that state's leadership principle of centralized decision making. In these cases, the church does not attempt to do the state's job by declaring that the state's policies are manifestly unjust—though Barth clearly thought that they were. The church simply declares what the church will not accept. "We reject the false teaching that the state could and should, beyond its specific function, become the sole order of human life and so also fulfill the role of the church. We reject the false teaching that beyond its specific function the church could and should take on the style, duties, and honors of a state and thus itself become an organ of the state."

Freedom and the Life of Faith

The freedom of the church to order its own life, which the Synod of Barmen made so clear with respect to the state, also appears with respect to other social institutions in Barth's later writings on ethics. To listen to the one Word of God, to trust and obey "Jesus Christ as he is witnessed to us in Holy Scripture" does not stop with the relationship of church and state, crucial though that was in the time of Nazi *Gleich-schaltung*. Obedience transforms our relationships to other institutions as well.

In Barth's later, more systematic work, these other social institutions appear as "definite spheres and relationships"[31] in human life. These spheres, which include worship, the family, the life of the body, and work in one's calling, are comparable to Brunner's orders of creation but with an important difference: the command of God is not found *within* the constraints and structures of the spheres. The command is, rather, addressed to persons who live in the spheres by God, who transcends these relationships and cannot be captured within their limits. Barth, of course, would never allow the command of God to be reduced to a simple, changeless code of rules, but he did observe that throughout the long history of Christianity, the path of obedience has followed certain "prominent lines."[32]

The intense concern to preserve God's freedom which dominates Barth's early work yields in the later writings to a more subtle awareness that freedom, even for God, must be the freedom to act, to do something with definitive consequences for the future. The important fact about God's sovereign freedom is that God has freely chosen the church as the place to make divine glory known to humanity. To insist that no human expectations can hold for divine freedom is to reduce it to a mere formal possibility and to deny God the freedom to do what God has in fact done: chosen a people in Jesus Christ. No law of reason could require that choice, nor can any general rule define its consequences, but the choice is for Barth nonetheless the heart of Christian ethics, and it leads to certain valid expectations of ourselves, of others, and of the commands of God. The continuing covenantal relationship between God who commands and the church which obeys leads us to expect a future consistent with the past and immediately calls into question anyone who claims a Word from God that falls outside these lines.[33] The concept of prominent lines thus provides a relatively secure knowledge in matters of obedience to God's commandments.

From the beginning the God who speaks to the church in Jesus calls them to hold their possessions loosely and to free themselves from attachments that might hinder their responsiveness to the kingdom of God. "But if anyone would see you and take your coat, let him have your cloak as well" (Matt. 5:40). "Leave the dead to bury their own dead; but as for you, go and proclaim the kingdom of God" (Luke

9:60). These commandments are not rules that we can simply apply to situations and then do what the rule says, but they give us some indication what we may expect when we truly hear the Word that God addresses to us.

Obedience as Barth conceives it is thus something quite different from the "critical cooperation" with the orders of creation that marks Brunner's idea of Christian vocation. The aim of obedient action is not the preservation and perfection of the orders but the proclamation to all that God has chosen humanity and called us to acknowledge that choice in covenant partnership. As obedience must not recognize "other events and powers, concepts and truths in addition to and beside the one Word of God,"[34] so it must not serve any secondary purposes which correspond to the aims of those other powers. Indeed, the "prominent lines" which Barth discerns in Jesus' commands seem to be set against the requirements of the orders. Where the orders require a firm commitment to family life, Jesus proclaims a liberation from "captivity to the clan."

> There can be no doubt that in its fear of the bogey of monasticism, Protestantism has very radically ignored this proclamation of Jesus Christ, as also that of other freedoms. To a very large extent it has acted as though Jesus had done the very opposite and proclaimed this attachment—the absolute of the family. Can we really imagine a single one of the prophets or apostles in the role of the happy father, or grandfather, or even uncle? . . . They may well have occupied this role. But in the function in which they are seen by us they stand outside these connexions.[35]

What is true of the family is equally true in the other orders of labor, culture, government, and religion. Where Brunner would call us to sustain and stabilize the ordinary patterns that enrich human life, Barth finds "prominent lines" in Jesus' commandments that call this ordinariness into question. Discipleship is not a matter of thoughtless nonconformity, but neither does it take the form of actions that will readily make sense to ordinary good people who live with us in the wider human society.

In what sense, then, is the church's obedience to the Word of God a public ethic? Is it possible that a pattern of action that begins with attention to the church's own Scripture and follows lines that run counter to all ordinary practical wisdom can nonetheless engage the understanding in ways that will lead others to recognize what obedience requires as a moral claim?

Certainly Barth's later writings allow us to establish more definite expectations about Christian action. It is no longer quite true that the Christian may be "a realist or an idealist . . . a Pietist, perhaps, but quite as well a communist. . . ."[36] Though there are no rules that say where Christians must be found, it is predictable that they will be among those who reject the imperatives of fame, wealth, and power and give themselves to meeting their neighbors' needs without anxiety over their own position. The command of God for each situation must be obeyed in the moment, but the main directions of Christian action are predictable.

To be predictable, however, is not quite the same thing as to make a moral claim. Predictability does have implications for action. If Christians are likely to behave in ways that show indifference to worldly success and a certain freedom from ordinary patterns of authority, people will take note of that and adjust their own behavior accordingly. If others are to treat this Christian behavior as a moral commitment and as a moral claim on their own lives, however, the Christian's action must be understandable, rather than merely predictable. To be sure, the world has a certain admiration for those quixotic spirits who enhance the lives of others without ever securing their own dreams for themselves. There is, too, a genuine form of honor reserved for those who, like Mother Teresa of Calcutta, have shown a consistent readiness to forego all ordinary recognition in order to serve those who can give nothing in return. Mother Teresa, who takes the homeless, dying poor from the city's streets and gives them a place to die with dignity and human care, has been honored with medals, degrees, and a Nobel Peace Prize, in no small measure because of her apparent indifference to such honors. Those who are admired or honored in this way are, however, rarely understood. Their actions carry no further than their own commitments, unless they also find ways to explain their causes, enlist others in their support, and transform society's rules into arrangements that are more compatible with their own aspirations. A hospice for the dying is not a medical center for the poor, as critics of Mother Teresa are quick to point out.[37]

A reader sympathetic to Barth might object at this point that the examples of obedience Barth had in mind were not inconspicuous acts of humble kindness. The obedience he envisioned was above all the obedience of Barmen, which set aside considerations of personal peace and security to take up a dangerous opposition to the reorganization of the German churches along Nazi lines. The obedience of the Confessing Church was carefully planned, thoroughly discussed, and publicly declared. No one can guarantee that such efforts will produce public acceptance, but how could the Synod have done more to secure public understanding?

The objection is well taken as a comment on the actions of the Synod, but we have already seen how Barth interprets such deliberations. The proceedings of a synod are a matter internal to the church, a "discernment of the spirits" rather than a discussion of public issues. Consideration begins with the testimony of Scripture and ends, not with declarations that have a wisdom apparent on rational grounds, but with the testimony of conscience, that knowing-with-God (con-scientia) in which Christians find assurance that their conclusions are right, even as they know that they can never possess and deliver the evidence for this certainty.[38]

In what sense, then, are these acts of obedience in the community of faith also acts of public ethics? Where does the implication of "God's powerful claim over the whole of our life"[39] reach beyond the lives of those who are committed to obedience and touch the structures of society generally? Clearly the point cannot be that discipleship embodies the true forms of government or work or family life. Discipleship serves precisely to free us from bondage to those expectations, even when the expectations are "religious" in the usual sense of that word. To be a good husband, father, grandfather, or uncle—to be a good magistrate, a good worker, or even a good priest—these things may be praiseworthy in human terms, but to return to the language of *The Epistle to the Romans,* "in no sense can they be even a first step toward the Kingdom of Heaven."[40] Discipleship will not explain itself or vindicate itself in any terms that society generally gives as reasons for action.

Unless such discipleship is to be a realm distinctly apart, indistinguishable to ordinary observers from eccentric vegetarian cultists and communal groups of admirable but ineffective idealists, we must take some pains to identify its import for the wider society. The Confessing Church which met at Barmen clearly meant to be more than a gathering of harmless mystics, but it is not immediately clear from Barth's account what more it can be.

The answer Barth had in mind seems to be something like this: the church makes a moral claim, an understandable claim, with implications for the actions of others, by claiming its freedom to follow the one Word of God in Jesus Christ. The church neither asks nor expects that the Word will be understood, but the freedom it requires for itself to follow the Word of God is perfectly comprehensible. The church, as Dietrich Bonhoeffer put it, "takes up space" in the world.[41] It is not a body of ideas that makes no claims for itself but a body of persons who demand conditions under which they may live out their faith. The church must be free, as the Barmen Declaration said, to order its own life and establish its own forms of leadership. The church must be free, as Barth later suggested, from "captivity to the clan," from excessive care for worldly recognition, and from the neurotic insistence that everything it does must somehow serve the efficient, orderly functioning of society.

A church which has this freedom does not write theological prescriptions for how the state or the society in general might best be organized. Barth perhaps overstepped the bounds of his own system when he wrote that "we are justified, from the point of view of exegesis, in regarding the 'democratic conception of the state' as a justifiable expansion of the thought of the New Testament." The church is not in the business of inventing ideal states or enlisting persons to work for their realization.[42] Yet this church, which is free to follow its Lord, by the mere fact of its existence sets some limits on the state and perhaps on other social institutions as well. The church can live in many types of society, but it obviously cannot be free in a state that "beyond its specific function, [seeks to] become the sole and total order of human life and so also fulfill the role of the church."[43] The church can live in many economic systems—capitalist, perhaps, but quite as well socialist—but it cannot be free in any system which binds the people solely to standards of material productivity and efficiency, no matter how production may be organized. The church can live with many forms of family life—the loving nurture of the nuclear family, perhaps, but quite as well the thoughtful cooperation of two parents who are no longer married or the shared responsibility of extended families—but the church cannot be free in any system which so binds persons' identity and sense of worth to their function in a family unit that they can no longer risk those ties in obedience to the demands of the Word of God.

Barth's aim, then, was not a political church or a church that would be a center for social reform. Barth's aim was a church that would simply and solely be true to its Lord. Yet that fidelity demands a freedom that is a public moral claim, a freedom that calls for understanding by others and has implications for their own actions. The church that Barth envisioned at Barmen was a church which by being true to its Lord not only proclaims ultimate salvation for all but also presently and very concretely assures freedom for all.

Barth's commitment to this idea of the church led to his dismissal from his professorship in Bonn, and that in turn sharply limited his further participation in the life of the Confessing Church in Germany. While his subsequent writings clearly show the imprint of the Confessing Church experience on his thinking about church and society, he was spared a personal confrontation with the most difficult question that arose in the aftermath of Barmen: Suppose that this church fails? Suppose that in attempting to adhere to the sole authority of the Word of God, the church loses sight of Christ's lordship over all areas of life and lapses into such exclusive concern with internal issues that it no longer "takes up space" in the world, that its freedom no longer makes moral claims on the actions of others? That issue was left for a new generation to face, a generation represented especially well by Dietrich Bonhoeffer.

NOTES

1. *Gleichschaltung* is a German noun that means, roughly, *coordination* or *bringing into line.* The National Socialists used the term to describe a process of reorganization through which all German institutions were to receive a centralized leadership comparable to the centralized organization of the Nazi state.

2. The Confessing Church (*Bekennende Kirche*) was the name used by those German Protestants who maintained their loyalty to the historic Protestant confessions of faith and refused to accept the reorganization of the churches prescribed by the Nazi government.

3. From the theological declaration adopted by the Confessing Church at Barmen in May 1934. A complete study of this declaration follows later in this chapter.

4. Eberhard Busch, *Karl Barth,* trans. John Bowden (Philadelphia: Fortress Press, 1976), 209–13.

5. Cf. Barth, *The Holy Ghost,* 81–82.

6. On this period generally, see Ernst C. Helmreich, *The German Churches Under Hitler* (Detroit: Wayne State University Press, 1979), 240–56.

7. For the text of the synod documents, see Heinrich Hermelink, ed., *Kirche im Kampf* (Tübingen: Rainer Wunderlich, 1950). The best English account of the synod is Arthur Cochrane, *The Church's Confession Under Hitler* (Philadelphia: Westminster, 1962). Cochrane also presents excellent English translations of the major documents.

8. Quoted in Busch, *Karl Barth,* 245.

9. Cochrane, *The Church's Confession,* 56–60. Cochrane notes that Barth had expressed this idea publicly as early as 1925.

10. For the German text see Hermelink, *Kirche im Kampf,* 110–13.

11. Cochrane, *The Church's Confession,* 254.

12. The analysis that follows is based on Barth's comments in his article,

"Barmen," in *Bekennende Kirche: Martin Niemöller zum 60. Geburtstag* (Munich: Kaiser Verlag, 1952), 9–17.

13. See chapter 3, 46.

14. See chapter 4, 82–83.

15. Martin Luther, "Secular Authority: To What Extent It Should Be Obeyed," in *Martin Luther: Selections from His Writings*, ed. John Dillenberger (Garden City, N.Y.: Doubleday Anchor Books, 1961), 370.

16. Barth, "Barmen," 14.

17. The remark is in a letter written in 1968, quoted in Busch, *Karl Barth*, 248.

18. Karl Barth, "Church and State," in *Community, State, and Church*, ed. Will Herberg (Gloucester, Mass.: Peter Smith, 1968), 101–48.

19. Col. 1:16.

20. Barth, "Church and State," 114–15.

21. Ibid., 119–20.

22. Ibid., 145.

23. Ibid., 143.

24. Three of these letters were published in the United States under the title *This Christian Cause* (New York: Macmillan Co., 1941).

25. Barth, "Church and State," 138.

26. Ibid., 139.

27. Shortly before World War II broke out in September 1939, Barth privately urged ecumenical leaders to call on Christians in Germany to oppose the war by refusing military service or even by sabotage. See Busch, *Karl Barth*, 298. Publicly, however, Barth urged armed force against the Hitler regime only by calling Christians to military service in the countries at war with Germany. Barth does not preclude active resistance to the state, however, where "the repressing of tyranny and the shedding of innocent blood can be carried out in no other way." See Karl Barth, *The Knowledge of God and the Service of God*, trans. J. L. M. Haire and Ian Henderson (London: Hodder & Stoughton, 1938), 217–32.

28. Karl Barth, *Against the Stream: Shorter Post-War Writings 1946–1952* (New York: The Philosophical Library, 1954). See also Karl Barth, *How to Serve God in a Marxist Land,* ed. Robert McAfee Brown (New York: Association Press, 1959).

29. This political theology is associated especially with the work of the Catholic author, Johannes B. Metz. See his *Faith in History and Society* (New York: Seabury Press, 1980).

30. Karl Barth, "Christian Community and Civil Community," in Herberg, *Community, State, and Church,* 165. This essay was first published just after World War II. It comments extensively on the fifth article of the Barmen Declaration.

31. Barth, *Church Dogmatics*. 3/4, 29–31.

32. Ibid., 4/2, 547.

33. Barth grew more emphatic on this point as the years passed. See Karl Barth, *The Christian Life*. This volume is a translation of classroom lectures which Barth intended to use in preparing the section on ethics for *Church*

Dogmatics, 4. The work was never completed, but the material published in *The Christian Life* may be taken as a statement of Barth's late views on ethics.

34. Barmen Declaration, Article 1.

35. Barth, *Church Dogmatics,* 4/2, 551.

36. Barth, *The Holy Ghost,* 82.

37. Jack A. Jennings, "A Reluctant Demurrer on Mother Teresa," *Christian Century,* 11 March 1981, 258–60.

38. Barth, "Church and State," 121.

39. Barmen Declaration, Article 2.

40. Barth, *Epistle,* 517.

41. Dietrich Bonhoeffer, *The Cost of Discipleship* (New York: Macmillan Co., 1959), 223.

42. Karl Barth, "Christian Community," 160.

43. Barmen Declaration, Article 3.

6
DIETRICH BONHOEFFER:
RESPONSIBILITY AND RESTORATION

Unlike Barth and Brunner, Bonhoeffer experienced the dislocations in European society after 1914 as the background of his life, and
not as a strange intrusion that called his theology into question. From
the beginning, however, he sensed that his teachers in the eminent
theological faculty at the University of Berlin were too set in the
theological patterns of the nineteenth century to meet the questions of
the postwar world. His own intellectual development was influenced by
reading Kierkegaard and Nietzsche, critics of the nineteenth century
systems, and by the new existentialist philosophy of Martin Heidegger.
His theological work responded more to Barth and Brunner than to
the historical studies of his teachers.

Bonhoeffer treats the structures of society in a way reminiscent of
the orders of creation in Brunner. He tries to identify the systems
around which life must be organized and treats ethics primarily as a
matter of cooperation in the proper functioning of those systems. Yet
there is a significant difference with Brunner, which becomes apparent
already in Bonhoeffer's lectures on Genesis in 1932 and 1933. These
orders (*Ordnungen*—he uses the word that Barth avoids) are not orders
of creation, but "orders of preservation." They do not reveal God's
original will for humanity, but they show us how, after the Fall, God
preserves us from the worst consequences of our sin. "All the orders of
our fallen world are God's orders of preservation on the way to Christ.
. . . They have no value in themselves."[1]

Characteristically, Bonhoeffer addresses the same problems that
Brunner studied, but he speaks to them with Barth's emphasis on
command and obedience. Where Brunner says that actions undertaken out of respect for the orders of creation are at the same time
actions in the kingdom of God, Bonhoeffer, in the early chapters of his

Ethics, emphasizes the difference between Christian action and ordinary moral deliberations.[2] Usually, moral decisions result from discussions about problems and cases, rules and applications. Christian ethics is the simplicity of obedient response to the Word of God. This does not mean that the Word is always evident or easy to discern, but it does imply that the norm for right action is simple and singular.[3] The problem for Bonhoeffer's ethics, then, was to retain the fundamental principle that "The Good is simply and solely the will of God,"[4] giving that principle normative status without excluding non-Christians from the moral discussion, making decisions about the will of God for a whole society without reducing the principle to a vague theological affirmation that leaves concrete moral decisions untouched.

Teacher in the Confessing Church

Bonhoeffer was a young lecturer on the theological faculty in Berlin when the struggle for control of the German churches began in 1933. He participated actively in the campaign that preceded the church elections in July, and he joined in the call for a synod that would decisively settle the issue of *Gleichschaltung* in the churches. In October 1933 Bonhoeffer accepted a position as pastor of a German congregation in London, so he had no part in the deliberations at Barmen the following spring. He remained an active participant in the Confessing Church movement, however, arranging minor embarrassments for the new leaders of the Reich church and running up an enormous bill for telephone calls and cables back to Germany. (The British Post Office eventually forgave a part of this sum.)

In 1935 Bonhoeffer returned to Germany to run a seminary for the Confessing Church. His first class of ordinands assembled in April, and by summer they were settled in an old boarding school at Finkenwalde, a village not far from the Baltic Sea. By this time Bonhoeffer was already drawn into the circle of officers and highly placed civilians who would become the leaders of the conspiracy against Hitler. Nevertheless, in the rural isolation of Finkenwalde, he taught his students a view of the church that centered on the Christian community of worship and discernment.[5] While he trained them for a ministry that would be tested by the state's hostility, he did not train them for resistance.

It seems, then, that Bonhoeffer worked at first to create the Confessing Church that Barth had envisioned. His church did not push a political program or assert itself it matters of social policy generally, but it was a church which "takes up space."[6] It demanded consideration for its own place in society and independence to conduct its own affairs, and that insistence in itself put some limits on the state. The Confessing Church's attentiveness to ministry belied the claims of the Reich church government and the Nazi state that there could be no center of order and authority apart from the new order inaugurated by Adolf Hitler.

How well that experiment worked is still a subject for discussion. To be sure, the Confessing Church lasted to the end of the Second World War and preserved throughout some measure of financial and organizational independence. More than the labor unions, or the press, or the universities, the Confessing Church resisted Nazi regimentation, and though its leaders and its members suffered, it did survive and its witness was noted. Albert Einstein spoke for many in Germany when he said:

> Only the Church stood squarely across the path of Hitler's campaign for suppressing the truth. I never had any special interest in the Church before, but now I feel a great affection and admiration for it, because the Church alone had had the courage and persistence to stand for intellectual and moral freedom.[7]

Nevertheless, the Confessing Church's single-minded focus on internal issues narrowed the impact of its witness. The consensus which united the Confessing Church did not encompass the broader social issues of the persecution of Jews and political dissidents. While this helped to demonstrate the Barmen thesis that the church cannot be the state, it contributed to a self-centeredness that Barth himself began to question: The Confessing Church "has as yet shown no sympathy for the millions who are suffering injustice. She has not once spoken out on the most simple matters of public integrity. And if and when she does speak, it is always on her own behalf."[8]

Restricting the Confessing Church's public demands to a defense of its own independence also allowed its less militant leaders to press for compliance with most of the government's orders on grounds of obedience to the legitimate power of the state. Under pressure all but the most important issues of theology and church order could be surrendered. After 1937 a more lenient attitude on the part of the government combined with a surge of popular patriotism to evoke a conciliatory mood among many Confessing Church leaders. While the church continued to "take up space," it took up less and less space as the Second World War approached. In 1938 a majority of Confessing pastors took an oath of loyalty to Hitler, and the Confessing Church councils generally endorsed their move, arguing that the oath was required out of respect for the authority of the state. Only when this surrender to authority was complete did the state attempt to convert it into a voluntary affirmation, announcing that the loyalty oath had been from the beginning an internal issue in the church and that the oath was not required.[9]

Agent of the Conspiracy

Bonhoeffer viewed these developments with mounting dissatisfaction, and although he remained in the ministry of the Confessing Church to the end of his life, he sought out other ways to act on his convictions. In 1940 he became a civilian agent for the *Abwehr*, German military intelligence. Ostensibly, he was to use his ecumenical contacts to obtain useful information. In fact, he was joining a group of officers and lawyers who planned to overthrow Hitler and use their foreign contacts to negotiate a peace settlement with the Allies. Although the conspirators rejected Hitler's expansionist war aims, they wanted desperately to avoid a peace like that of 1919, which placed Germany at the mercy of the victors and aroused resentments that eventually brought Hitler to power. Bonhoeffer's special role in the conspiracy was to contact the British government through an English bishop, George Bell, whom he was able to meet in Sweden in 1942. The conspirators sought some signal that if the Hitler regime were replaced, the Allies might reduce their demand for Germany's unconditional surrender. The British government decided to ignore the message.[10]

Germany's bleak military prospects and a growing awareness within the inner circle of conspirators of the full horror of Hitler's "final solution" for the Jews sustained the conspiracy even in the face of Allied indifference. Bonhoeffer and several of his closest associates were arrested in April 1943 for their connection with a plot to help several Jews escape from Germany through Switzerland.[11] He was never formally tried apart from a summary hearing the night before his death. The authorities did not suspect the full extent of the conspiracy until after an attempt on Hitler's life failed on July 20, 1944. By that time, of course, Bonhoeffer had already been imprisoned for more than a year. His captivity continued until he was executed in April 1945, a few weeks before the collapse of the Third Reich.

Bonhoeffer's dramatic role in the conspiracy was accompanied by a struggle to formulate a theological response to the changed situation. In the decisive controversy within the Confessing Church over the loyalty oath, the pastors who spoke of obedience to state authority had significantly misjudged their adversary. What the state wanted from the church was not obedience but endorsement. The oath was legally unimportant. What mattered was that it could be twisted into a spontaneous expression of support for Hitler and presented that way in propaganda. Helmut Thielicke has aptly summarized the use of the oath as a tool to legitimate the Nazi regime:

> Corruption in the meaning of oaths reached a climax under National Socialism because the ceremonial oath was regarded primarily from the standpoint of its propagandistic power of suggestion. It was merely an exercise whose value consisted in the degree of its repetition.[12]

Bonhoeffer understood this issue more clearly than most. As early as 1933 he recognized that the totalitarianism emerging in Germany was different from the traditional forms of authority that have stood alongside of or against the church.

> There is a decisive difference between the authority of the father, the teacher, the judge and the statesman on the one hand, and the authority of the Leader (*Führer*) on the other. The former have their authority by virtue of their office and by virtue of that office alone; the Leader has authority by virtue of his person. The authority of the former can be attacked and maimed, but it still remains; the authority of the Leader is utterly at the risk of every moment; it is in the hands of his followers.[13]

Clearly this problem of illegitimate, authoritarian power is rather different from the opposition between the established church and the legitimate state that Barth had in mind when he called for a church that would make its witness by steadfast obedience to its own nonpolitical source of authority. The theoretical task for Bonhoeffer was to explain precisely how the situation was different and to explain the changed structure of moral action which follows.

A New Approach to Ethics

Bonhoeffer's reflections on his wartime work appear chiefly in his *Ethics.* The book was never completed, and the parts that we do have were written in intervals which the pressure of events permitted. Bonhoeffer's thoughts are sometimes not fully developed, nor are they always clear. The obscurity is perhaps deliberate. A man who seeks to overthrow his own government in wartime can hardly go about with a theological notebook on the subject. We must sometimes read between the lines of the *Ethics* to see what Bonhoeffer had in mind. Nevertheless, the main lines of a new treatment of the subject can be seen in chapters 5 through 7 of Part 1.

Bonhoeffer begins with close attention to the orders of creation or orders of preservation, which he now calls "divine mandates."[14] The new term stresses the point that human responsibilities for labor, marriage, government, church, and culture are tasks imposed by God, not merely functional requirements of society or patterns set for us by nature. Bonhoeffer had previously expressed a new appreciation for "the natural," which he noted had become a suspect category in Protestant ethics.[15] The important patterns of development which human life naturally follows are incorporated into the concept of a divine mandate, but Bonhoeffer is now convinced that the specific forms the mandates have taken in the West cannot be fully explained as universal features of natural human development. In the West we have an attitude toward our institutions that distinguishes us from other peoples and periods. We understand laws and customs in terms of historical development, not timeless myths, and we are aware that reason and technology have given us enormous power to shape that historical inheritance for the future. These ideas have penetrated all cultures to some extent in modern times, as Bonhoeffer recognized, but their widespread acceptance today does not change their origins in a particular part of human history. They are not simply another variation on unchanging structures of human life such as Brunner tried to discern in the orders of creation. Indeed, modern institutions shaped by history and technology cannot be understood at all apart from the unique event that makes our ideas about history, technology, and historical changes possible.

> The concept of historical inheritance, which is linked with the consciousness of temporality and opposed to all mythologization, is possible only where thought is consciously or unconsciously governed by the entry of God into history at a definite place and a definite point of time, that is to say, by the incarnation of God in Jesus Christ. . . . Consequently, when we ask about the historical inheritance we are not asking the timeless question of those values of the past of which the validity is eternal. Man himself is set in history and it is for that reason that he asks himself about the present and about the way the present is taken up by God in Christ.[16]

When Bonhoeffer speaks of preserving the heritage of the West or describes the church as the "bearer of a historical inheritance . . . bound by an obligation to the historical future,"[17] he is not effecting a union of faith and human values such as might have appealed to his older professors in Berlin and would surely have appalled Karl Barth. It is not that reason confirms the truths of faith but rather that the truths of reason are encompassed by a definitive historical reality. To the extent that we attempt to speak of human values, the institutions that sustain them, and the lines of authority that make institutions work in timeless terms, apart from the reality of Christ, our ethics will be abstract—universally valid, perhaps, but too general to help us make specific decisions. Bonhoeffer calls his alternative to abstraction "ethics as formation."

> Ethics as formation, then, means the bold endeavour to speak about the way in which the form of Jesus Christ takes form in our world, in a manner which is neither abstract nor casuistic, neither programmatic nor purely speculative.[18]

Obedience

It is the unity of the mandates in Christ which allows us to live with what would otherwise be a multiplicity of conflicting obligations. Our experience of life is that the demands of family often compete with the demands of labor and that caring about what happens to a child or a spouse may make us less attentive to our work. Efficiency and optimum utilization of resources may lead to a sterile, mechanized environment that is devoid of beauty and tradition; so the demands of labor compete with the demands of culture. Also, as the Confessing Church knew very well, the demands of a certain sort of government will compete with the claims of the church. With the pain and dissension that the uncoordinated mandates can cause, it is little wonder that an era that has largely forgotten Christ would seek to eliminate the complexity and end the conflict by making one mandate supreme and ignoring the claims of all the others. The totalitarian state represents this solution, but so, in a gentler way, does an exclusive devotion to family, and so does the maxim that "what's good for General Motors is good for America." Even an exclusive devotion to the church can become a kind of ecclesiastical totalitarianism that ignores the other ways that Christ takes form in the world.

In fact, there is an irreducible multiplicity to the claims upon us, a multiplicity which is evident in the variety of the mandates themselves. Those who bear this truth in mind must not, however, think that they can bring an easy unity to the demands by deciding for themselves which mandate takes priority or appealing to general principles to settle potential conflicts. It is rather a matter of listening attentively to what is actually required of us in the moment. "Decision and action can no longer be delegated to the personal conscience of the individual. Here there are concrete commandments and instructions for which obedience is demanded."[19] The potential conflicts between the mandates are numerous; but where the mandates themselves are rightly ordered and we are attentive to the concrete, specific commandments, the actual result should be harmonious, a cooperation between the various spheres of obligation that shape our lives which no merely theoretical ordering could accomplish.

No private inspiration, no supratemporal concept of human good that hovers above the mandates without becoming concrete in any one of them can be the commandment of God. What the commandment establishes in each of the mandates, however, is not so much a natural order as a chain of command.

> This means that the commandment of God does not spring from the created world. It comes down from above. It does not arise from the factual claim on men of earthly powers and laws, from the claim of the instinct of self-preservation or from the claim of hunger, sex, or political force. It stands beyond all these as a demand, a precept, and judgment. The commandment of God establishes on earth an inviolable superiority and inferiority which are independent of the factual relations of power and weakness.[20]

It is this ordering of superior and inferior that provides the concreteness of the divine mandates. Before we can know what we are to do, we must know to whom we are to listen. Ethical discourse, the setting of moral requirements and making decisions about what ought to be done, is not a task to be undertaken by just anyone who thinks he or she understands the situation. Ethical discourse requires an authorization from the command which establishes the "inviolable superiority and inferiority which are independent of the factual relations of power and weakness." One who would issue commands must have, in Bonhoeffer's vivid imagery, a "warrant" (*Ermächtigung*)—a warrant for ethical discourse.[21]

This warrant is the "decisive difference" that distinguishes the authority of the father, teacher, or judge from that of the political leader who rules by popular acclaim. Those who truly possess the warrant for ethical discourse do not need continual affirmation of their power, for their authority comes finally from the one Authority to whom all the mandates are subordinated. "The bearer of the mandates acts as a deputy in place of Him who assigns him his commission."[22] This legitimate authority does not depend on the skill or the success of the one who holds it. "The master craftsman is still the master even for his talented journeyman, and the father is still the father even for his worthy and meritorious son. Quite independently of the subjective side of the matter, it is still the master and the father who possess the warrant for ethical discourse."[23] Yet just because it is independent of human skill and subjective preference, the warrant for ethical discourse is limited. It applies to offices, not to the people who occupy them. It gives authority over certain tasks, not a comprehensive power to order others about and to dispose of their lives according to one's own plan. No one can claim the role of the all-powerful leader, for the warrant for that discourse does not exist. Neither, therefore, can we choose such a leader for ourselves, however much we might want one in our fear and confusion. What characterizes the divine mandates is orderly division of authority *among* the different mandates and proper relations of superior and inferior *within* each of them.

Responsibility and Restoration

Bonhoeffer's idea of the mandates also gives him a fresh view of the period of crisis that followed World War I and led Germany to Hitler's Reich and a second global conflict. Hitler's power marks the failure of the mandates and a breakdown of the structure of superior and subordinate in separate and distinct patterns of authority. The controversy that gave rise to the Confessing Church exemplifies this, for there the church suffered both the intrusion of the state into its mandate and the internal disruption of its order by the enforced centralization that all but wiped out the regional authorities of the *Landeskirchen*.

The church, however, does not suffer alone. The mandate of the family has surrendered parental authority to the "revolution of youth" and an uncritical admiration for the ways of the young.[24] Labor and culture have endured "the spoilation and exploitation of the poor and the enrichment and corruption of the strong."[25] It would be naive to blame Hitler for all of this, and Bonhoeffer recites the evidence of social decay, not as an accusation against the rulers, but as a confession of the church's guilt and complicity in this massive defection from the Christian heritage of the West.

Totalitarianism is a corruption of the state which is possible only because the other mandates are already weak and misguided. The Nazi program intrudes on family, church, and culture because these institutions no longer take their historic roles seriously. They are willing or even eager to surrender their authority to one who acts like he knows what to do with it. The Nazi state gains endorsement through loyalty oaths and displays its popularity in massive propaganda rallies because no one any longer trusts the quiet and natural authority of the parent in the home, the pastor in the pulpit, or the master craftsman in the workshop. If previous centuries knew nothing like this totalitarian state, that was not entirely because they lacked the technology that supports the Nazi repression. They also preserved a profound respect for the patterns of order in which—whether they knew it or not—Christ was taking form in the West. The unprecedented catastrophes of this century are signs that that respect and with it the structures of society as we have known them have collapsed. The cruel and distorted form of government we call totalitarianism has simply moved in to fill the vacuum.

> What the West is doing is to refuse to accept its historical inheritance for what it is. The West is becoming hostile toward Christ. This is the peculiar situation of our time, and it is genuine decay. . . . The world has known Christ and has turned its back on Him, and it is to this world that the Church must now prove that Christ is the living Lord.[26]

Against this epochal change, all the usual responses look slightly foolish. The optimism of the nineteenth century, which saw modern progress as the fulfillment of Christianity, is discredited, but so is that form of religious socialism which assumed that history would inevitably bring both capitalist exploiters and Nazi fanatics to the point of a genuine "socialist decision." Even Barth's exegetical delineation of the proper roles of church and state and the Catholic theory of government restrained by a framework of natural law seem pointless under the circumstances. Hitler established his own order of power in defiance of the order set forth in Scripture or discerned in nature, and for the moment the order of power has prevailed. Although Bonhoeffer could not have said it in writing, he must have been thinking of Hitler as he wrote an essay on success in 1940:

> The world will allow itself to be subdued only by success. It is not ideas or opinions which decide, but deeds. Success alone justifies wrongs done. Success heals the wounds of guilt. There is no sense in reproaching the successful man for his unvirtuous behavior, for this would be to remain in the past while the successful man strides forward from one deed to the next, conquering the future and securing the irrevocability of what has been done. The successful man presents us with accomplished facts which can never again be reversed. What he destroys cannot be restored. What

he constructs will acquire at least a prescriptive right in the next generation. . . . The judges of history play a sad role in comparison with its
protagonists. History rides roughshod over their heads.[27]

In the face of massive historical dislocations, a reassertion of the
Word of God or the law of nature will not by itself make obedience to
those imperatives possible. What the world requires is a restoration of
the mandates. Guides that tell us what to do and whom to obey within a
framework of order are useless when the framework itself has collapsed, and for Bonhoeffer the evidences of that collapse were so
apparent that previous Christian ethics, right down to the pronouncements of the Confessing Church and Barth's magisterial essay on the
"discernment of spirits" in political life, begin to appear as theoretical
elaborations of an order that no longer exists.

To restore an order in which such studies might once again make
sense requires the same sort of resolute action by which the decaying
order had been displaced. "It is not ideas or opinions which decide, but
deeds." From the middle of 1940 onwards, the *Abwehr* conspiracy had
made specific plans to change the government of Germany and, if
necessary, to kill Hitler to do it. This undertaking, which eventually
cost Bonhoeffer his life, was not for him an act of obedience, but a
"venture of responsibility."[28] The venture of responsibility takes place
in a situation in which ordinary moral demands provide no guidance.
Responsible action perhaps even violates ordinary moral expectations.
In this venture the course of action is determined by the exigencies of
history, not by constitutional principles or the decisions of synods. The
possibility of an individual decision, which seemed ruled out by the
obedience demanded at Barmen, now reappears as an inescapable
necessity. When the Confessing Church leaders closest to Bonhoeffer
began to speak, reluctantly and certainly very quietly, about the possibility of resistance by the church, Bonhoeffer himself sat in silence.[29]
The resistance they wanted, a resistance justified by principles of faith
and enjoined as an act of Christian obedience, was not possible, but he
had already entered upon a responsible resistance about which he
could say nothing.

The Conspiracy

What Bonhoeffer wrote about the "venture of action" or the "venture of responsibility" was matched by the boldness of the plot. The
conspirators, many of them highly placed in the German government,
intended to kill Hitler and assume control of the state themselves as a

prelude to negotiating an end to the war on more favorable terms than the Allies would extend to a Nazi regime. The transformation contemplated was a revolution "from above," a return to power of the progressive elements among the aristocratic officers and intellectuals who had shaped German culture before the collapse of the old Empire. When the conspirators drafted an announcement to be issued after the coup, they made it clear that they wanted no repetition of the popular upheavals of 1919. "Everyone must continue to do his duty wherever he is, obeying only the laws and decrees of the new authority. The destiny of our hard-fighting soldiers depends on everyone's giving his utmost on the home front."[30]

The conspirators proclaimed their intention to restore government based on law and put an end to arbitrary, dictatorial powers. Still, in their own deliberations they could hardly ignore the fact that the Nazis governed with a semblance of legality. Hitler had been summoned to power by the President of the Republic in 1933 and confirmed by the majority of the German people in a parliamentary election a few weeks later. The emergency decrees by which Hitler gave himself virtually absolute power were based on explicit provisions of the Weimar constitution, and indeed his democratic predecessors had used the same provisions to govern during the waning days of the Republic.[31] There was a paradox in the conspirators' plan to resore a genuine legal order by an initial act of revolutionary violence against what remained of the old constitutional order, and this paradox could not be entirely resolved by the conspirators' proclamation that "we have taken over the power of the state, after having examined our consciences before God."[32]

There could be no doubt about the importance of what the conspirators planned to do for Germany's future, nor did they lack evidence of the evil and suffering wrought by Hitler's regime. Bonhoeffer fully supported the plot and its aims, but he nevertheless refused to dispose lightly of the moral problems involved in murdering a tyrant and acting against all lawful authority. He had no easy answer for those who drew back from assassination because of conscientious scruples against bloodshed nor for those who saw the plot itself as a violation of their military oath, a breach of honor which would discredit their character even if the conspiracy were to succeed.

Still less could Bonhoeffer excuse his own defection from the role of the pastor and the straightforward public witness which the Christian confession demanded. While the leaders of the Confessing Church did not know the full extent of his political involvement, Bonhoeffer knew that they would not have approved it; and he would not have been surprised that, after the War, some church leaders refused to number the "political martyr" Dietrich Bonhoeffer along with the Confessing Church members who had died in more open and purely religious acts of witness.[33] Later writers have objected to this criticism of Bonhoeffer and sought to justify his political activity as a legitimate Christian act, but Bonhoeffer himself would have understood the force of the theological objections.

> We have been silent witnesses of evil deeds; we have been drenched by many storms; we have learnt the arts of equivocation and pretence; experience has made us suspicious of others and kept us from being truthful and open; intolerable conflicts have worn us down and even made us cynical. Are we still of any use?[34]

The theologian who wrote so decisively of the commandment of God which is available only in the orderly patterns of authority established by the mandates could not easily excuse his own venture across the line that distinguishes the church from the state, nor could he treat as unimportant the violation of lines of command within the government itself. The possibility of obedience could be restored only by an act of disobedience, a violation, not only of human laws, oaths, and confidences, but in some measure the mandates themselves. To interpose an appeal to natural law or to a natural right to resist tyrants, to appeal legalistically to conditions that might invalidate the military oath and abrogate the obligation to obey would create an illusion of justification that would only distract from the seriousness of what the conspirators proposed to do.

Action that makes obedience possible once again, action that restores an order in which responsiveness to authority is at the same time moral action within the mandates God provides requires the forcible assumption of a warrant one does not possess. While legitimate authority may rightly use force to restrain evil, those who turn force against the power of a corrupt state are from the beginning corrupted themselves. There is no way to avoid this paradox, and no escape from the uneasy question which must arise for all who contemplate its results: "Are we still of any use?"

Bonhoeffer's answer was not a moral justification of the conspirators' actions but an appeal to God's justification of sinners. The risk in a venture of responsibility is more than the risk of detection and unpleasant punishments. In involves a moral risk to oneself, the risk that the venture will lead to a cynical, suspicious, and power-hungry approach to all human relationships in the future. No one who stands on record of personal moral perfection can undertake such a venture, but one who trusts all claims to personal righteousness to a forgiving God may find the venture worth the risk. "Civil courage, in fact, can grow only out of the free responsibility of free men. . . . It depends on a God who demands responsible action in a bold venture of faith and promises forgiveness and consolation to the man who becomes a sinner in that venture."[35]

Reflecting on his own participation in the conspiracy against Hitler, Bonhoeffer found a place within his ethical system for a "venture of responsibility" which was quite different from the act of obedience of Christians within the church which he had first sought, along with Barth and others, in the formation of the Confessing Church. The specifically Christian marks of obedience are largely absent from the venture of responsibility. It is an act based on a sound reading of the facts and a type of civil courage which can be shared with others; and yet, properly understood, the venture involves a risk of personal corruption so great that only one who believes in the power of a Christian grace is likely to undertake it.

Responsibility and Moral Duty

Bonhoeffer's insistence that ethics must be "concrete" and his rejection of general moral rules recalls Brunner's earlier account of the inadequacies of moral philosophy, but the idea of a venture of responsibility is not simply a theological critique of moral philosophy. Whatever the limitations of general moral rules and autonomous moral reason, Bonhoeffer realized that no modern theologian can turn away from them to create a completely theological ethic. "Contempt for the age of rationalism is a suspicious sign of failure to feel the need for truthfulness. If intellectual honesty is not the last word that is to be said about things, and if intellectual clarity is often achieved at the expense of insight into reality, this can still never again exempt us from the inner obligation to make clear and honest use of reason."[36]

Bonhoeffer's complaint is that all forms of ethics, philosophical and theological, are inadequate to the special situation that elicits a venture of responsibility. Ethicists make the mistake of responding to these unique historical opportunities by citing general rules because their systems are focused on ordinary moral situations, drawing attention to "the 'shall' and the 'should' which impinge on all life from its periphery."[37] Ethics calls attention to structures within which the hierarchy of command and obedience makes sense and elicits our cooperation through reasoned assent rather than mere force. That much is true of the ethics of the theologians, as well as the philosophers. What the systems ordinarily do not tell us, however, is what we must do when those structures no longer exist. The situation of responsibility is one in which we must create the conditions under which the moral life can be lived. The "shall" and the "should" cannot meaningfully be addressed to persons in the midst of life when the "periphery," the framework of order and legitimate authority, is not there. In that sense, the venture of responsibility seems to fall outside the scope of ethics altogether.

At the same time, Bonhoeffer says that God "demands" responsible action of us, by which he seems to integrate the venture that makes obedience possible back into the system of command and obedience itself. Perhaps the clearest way to think of Bonhoeffer's ethical system, then, is to see it as a form of deontology, an ethics of duty in which obedience is generally much more important than assessing the consequences of one's actions. Bonhoeffer's ethics of duty, like Barth's is an act-deontology. This is apparent in his criticism of general rules and of all attempts to substitute moral principles for contrete acts of obedience.

The concept of responsibility, however, introduces a teleological element that is missing in Barth's ethics of obedience and allows Bonhoeffer to endorse actions that Barth could never support. Bonhoeffer will not generalize about moral duties or displace the concrete commandment found in the patterns of superior and inferior that mark the divine mandates, but he acknowledges responsibility as the fundamental idea that unifies the moral life. "This concept of responsibility is intended as referring to the concentrated totality and unity of the response to the reality which is given to us in Jesus Christ, as distinct from the partial responses which might arise, for example, from a consideration of utility or from particular principles."[38] Unlike the utilitarian criterion of "the greatest good for the greatest number" or Kant's categorical imperative, the concept of responsibility does not tell us what must be done in particular cases. The "shall" and the "should" we encounter have to do with living out life as a parent or child, teacher or pupil, master or apprentice. Nevertheless, the fundamental idea, which for Barth would already be a dangerous falling away from the immediacy of obedience, gives Christians a unity in the understanding of their actions that is not immediately apparent in the diversity of the concrete commandments and the multiplicity of the mandates. "Responsibility means, therefore, that the totality of life is pledged and that our action becomes a matter of life and death."[39]

The seriousness of this commitment cannot be lightly set aside, even when the framework of order that provides the parameters of obedience is shaken. When the value of money becomes uncertain, family loyalties cannot be trusted, and genuine human needs are manipulated to satisfy a leader's political ambitions—all of which had happened in Germany in Bonhoeffer's time—then none of the mandates is a truly reliable guide to action, and those who cannot see beyond concrete, particular requirements will understandably conclude that the time for ethics is past and it is now every person for himself or herself. The Christian moral life is more tenacious, and while Christians also suffer in the disorders that follow when the mandates are neglected, they are not entirely without guidance. They are committed with their whole lives to a Lord whose yes and no, whose judgment and acceptance condition all their encounters and preclude selfish and unforgiving choices, even when the usual guidelines for action are no longer clear. "We 'live' when our encounter with men and with God, the 'yes' and the 'no' are combined in a unity of contradictions, in selfless self-assertion, in self-assertion in the sacrifice of ourselves to God and to men."[40]

Obedience remains central in Bonhoeffer's account of the moral life. He shares that emphasis with Barth, and he would never allow it to be replaced by an attempt to delineate the general requirements of responsibility. When concrete obedience becomes impossible, however, the fundamental concept of responsibility insures that Christians are not at a complete loss. What is still possible is to act decisively yet selflessly, so that in this particular historical situation we recreate the conditions that would once again allow obedience to the duties that fall upon us owing to our place in the mandates. To say that God demands responsible action of us means that when we are confronted by a moral crisis, our basic commitment is not to save our own lives but to risk and if necessary to lose them on behalf of others.

The "venture of responsibility," then, is not the whole of the moral life.[41] It arises when the usual forms of duty are impossible and we find ourselves confronted by a special conjunction of *task* and *opportunity*. Where the structure of the moral life is intact, where the mandates all function well and the pattern of authority and subordination within each mandate is maintained, there is no need for a disruptive venture of responsibility. Bonhoeffer in his *Ethics* does not share the sense of the theology of crisis that human institutions are always in a state of disorder that is simply seem more clearly in the crisis of modern times. He views his own time as an exception, one which calls for a venture of responsibility of heroic proportions but which must not mislead us into thinking that its peculiar task will always be with us. To approach every situation in life as though it called for a venture of responsibility would be to ignore the obligations that the persistent divine mandates impose on us. When we can follow the promptings of authorities in church, government, family, and culture, when these mandates work together in a harmony that bespeaks the lordship of Christ over all of them, then we certainly ought to avoid utopian attempts to substitute our own ideas for the order that already exists. Only when that order has decayed, when obedience to authority produces confusion or the lines of legitimate authority are no longer clear is responsible action needed.

Even then, responsible action may be impossible. We can be deprived of the opportunity to be responsible even when the task is clearly present. In a paper prepared for a Confessing Church commission that met shortly before his arrest in 1943, Bonhoeffer clearly envisioned the possibility that a hostile government could so restrict the church's activity as to deprive Christians of all secular responsibility. When Christians are identified as a group to be persecuted and excluded from power, we can hardly expect that they will wield much influence over the course of political events. While the task of creating the conditions for moral life then clearly exists, the church and those who are closely identified with the church will usually lack the opportunities for responsible action. Bonhoeffer's place in the conspiracy against Hitler was the result of his background and his extraordinary family connections. He seized that opportunity for himself, but at the same time he cautioned the Confessing Church against futile gestures of resistance that amounted to attempts to act responsibly when the opportunity was lacking. This was not an invitation for the church to slink into obscurity, for "even the congregation in the catacombs will never be deprived of the universality of its mission." When the state deprives the church of secular responsibility, however, the mission of the church becomes principally a matter of open proclamation and strict congregational discipline under the sufferings of persecution. "In preaching the law and the gospel, it openly professes this mission and so keeps in view its responsibility for the world."[42] In this extreme situation, in which the opportunity for responsible action is largely absent, Bonhoeffer assigns the church a role comparable to Barth's vision of the church that serves by sticking stubbornly to legitimate obedience in its own mandate and so proclaims its own freedom.

Responsibility and Re-Formation

Just as it is important for Bonhoeffer to specify the conditions under which the venture of responsibility is appropriate, so he is concerned to specify its purpose. A venture of responsibility requires more than an intent to make the best of the situation as we find it. It is a commitment to restructure the situation so that the laws inherent in the divine mandates can once again be effective.

> It is true that all historically important action is constantly overstepping the limits set by these laws. But it makes all the difference whether such overstepping of the appointed limits is regarded in principle as the superseding of them . . . or whether the overstepping is regarded as a fault which is perhaps unavoidable, justified only if the law and the limit are reestablished and respected as soon as possible.[43]

Bonhoeffer's aim is to bring back a pattern of authority that allowed an uncomplicated obedience and asked only a measured loyalty, a pattern that wartime deceit and Nazi demands for total obedience had destroyed.

The unavoidable question for those who live in other times and places is whether the concrete aims of Bonhoeffer's venture are adequate to their own needs. The tendency to remake Bonhoeffer's ethics into a situation ethics, to find in his writings a warrant for rethinking moral action along lines that seem to meet our needs at the moment, is in part an attempt to evade more direct confrontation with the rather conservative social ideas that dominate Bonhoeffer's description of the mandated order. A critic can find much that betrays the author's origins in the wealthy family of a German professor with a solid bourgeois background and connections to the old Prussian aristocracy. Much more seems questionable in light of subsequent social change, like the wedding sermon written for Eberhard Bethge and Bonhoeffer's niece, Renate Schleicher: "The place where God has put the wife is in the husband's home."[44] The specific conditions of life which Bonhoeffer hoped to create or to restore often share some of the defects we noted in the details of Brunner's orders of creation.[45] They are not universal, even in the Christian West, nor are they so purely a response to God's Word in Scripture as Bonhoeffer's sermons might suggest. Barth summed up his uneasiness with Bonhoeffer's vision of the Christian venture to restore a pattern of natural authority and honest obedience by asking, "In Bonhoeffer's doctrine of the mandates, is there not just a suggestion of North German patriarchalism? Is the notion of the authority of some over others really more characteristic of the ethical event than that of the freedom of even the very lowest before the very highest?"[46]

To understand Bonhoeffer's venture of responsibility, we must not dismiss these images of marriage, family, and culture. Neither can we ignore the frankly restorationist aims of those who plotted to remove Hitler and return political power to the professions and classes best trained to use it. Rather, we must penetrate through the details to the meaning they had in Bonhoeffer's theology, and there we may find some guidance for our own ventures.

Bonhoeffer's primary commitment was not to the details of life among the German academic bourgeoisie, deeply engrained as these were in his own personality. His commitment was to their historical meaning as the mandates in which Christ takes form in the world. The reality which he insists must guide our actions is more than a situational assessment of the possibilities of the moment, but it is also more than the heritage that Bonhoeffer knew in his family home and longed for in the isolation of prison. The reality which guides our actions encompasses both situation and heritage in the not yet visible reality of Christ, in whom alone the multiplicity of our obligations can be unified. In this Christocentric view of reality, no ordering of the mandates can claim the status of the original "natural" model to which all subsequent arrangements must return.

A society or a political system at a specific point in history is simply a more or less adequate attempt to balance the claims of the various mandates and to create conditions under which they each have appropriate authority. When such a system is disrupted by historical change or deliberate evil, there can be no question of putting things back the way they were. A modern industrial society precludes the relationships between master and apprentice that served the mandates of labor and culture in the medieval guild. The attempt to recreate them is a bit of sentimental romanticism, and what is worse from a theological point of view, it falsely identifies a specific, historical form, with faults and values appropriate to its place and time, with the Creator's original intention regarding human work.

Responsibility, then, is not so much restoration as it is *re-formation*.

Christ must begin to take form again in the structures of human life. The Christian does not seek to return to a former way of life. The Christian seeks to end the West's hostility toward Christ. Human life must take on a form that bespeaks God's acceptance of humanity. This happens precisely when concrete acts of obedience are possible, when persons can meet the demands they encounter every day in work, family, citizenship, and worship without becoming hopelessly divided within themselves and without being set at odds with their neighbors. Just how this is possible cannot be determined by specific patterns from the past, any more than it can be settled by reference to general rules. In disordered times the venture that restores order is most likely to be taken by those who remember something better, but they doom themselves to failure if their venture becomes an exercise in nostalgia. Re-formation begins when each of the mandates is free to do its work under *present* conditions, and true reformers must remember that the past at its best is only a partial, limited realization of the unity of life that formation in Christ aims to complete. Barth siad that the Christian has certainty of conscience "only eschatologically." Knowledge of what we are to do is only a moment of experience, never a permanent possession. Bonhoeffer puts the same limitation on our forms of social organization. We are aware, concretely, when obedience to the divine command in the mandates is possible, but we should never make the mistake of supposing that the possibility belongs to that particular arrangement and to no other. The conditions for the mandates to function must be assessed objectively and unsentimentally, and a Christian venture of responsibility will probably be set against anyone who simply wants to recreate the past. A restoration that is also a re-formation may impose new duties unknown before; it may extend opportunities and protections to those who never had them before; it may devise new services that meet human needs which formerly went untended. This imaginative power to envision new forms of social organization has always been important in Christian thought. It is particularly important, however, to give it due systematic weight in Bonhoeffer's ethics, lest his deep feeling for his own past distract us from the real import of his ethics.

The Scope of Responsibility

By intercession and proclamation, Christians make it clear that even in the most difficult times, they take responsibility for the life of the world in which Christ takes form in history. By their readiness to risk guilt and to depend on grace rather than self-justification, they are prepared better than others to seize the conjunction of task and opportunity that restores the possibility of obedience in the wider society. This readiness for the venture of responsibility must mark the Christian life at all times, but we cannot understand Bonhoeffer's own actions unless we remember that he regarded the actual exercise of responsibility as only a part of the moral life. The venture of responsibility is not the whole of morality, and it is not for everyone. Often, indeed, it seems that Bonhoeffer wanted to make these ventures quite rare. "They create a situation which is extraordinary; they are by nature peripheral and abnormal events."[47] After we have settled the question whether Bonhoeffer's often rather conservative German social vision speaks to us today, we must then ask whether Bonhoeffer *intends* to speak to us at all. Does he address the *Ethics* to those who live far from the centers of power and make their political choices in the ambiguities of ordinary times; or is his advice only to those whose birth, luck, and skill have put them at the center of events and entitled them to take a formative role in history?[48]

Perpetual responsibility is, of course, impossible. We cannot insist that everyone rethink the framework of action without lapsing into confusion, and we cannot experiment continually with revisions of the structures of society without lapsing into disorder. Nevertheless, the task of creating the conditions for a moral life arises, not only in dramatic confrontations with a totalitarian state, but also in quieter ways in the other mandates. Already in Bonhoeffer's time, but even more today, the changing role of women makes for changes in marriage and family life which cannot be handled simply by reasserting platitudes about traditional family roles. Patterns of authority must shift to accommodate the more equal economic roles of husband and wife and the involvement of each in the demands and pressures outside the home. Respect for parental guidance must now often extend to a parent's new spouse, involving parents, children, and stepparents in the tricky venture of creating a stable and sustaining home life without undermining respect and affection for a parent who is no longer a part of the household. Some of these conditions depend on courts and legislatures, but the task and opportunity for these ventures fall largely on those who are directly caught up in them.

Similar circumstances abound. Churches, like families, are caught up in the changing role of women, so that opportunities for ministry which seemed adequate when social roles in general were more sharply distinguished by gender no longer suffice. Concern over the relationships between productivity, incentive systems, and worker morale means that labor relations will nowhere be treated as a matter of course. American technology, Swedish and Yugoslav factory organization, and Japanese management techniques are studied, analyzed, and assembled in new combinations to create new patterns of appropriate action in the mandate of labor. In all of these situations, the churches share in shaping values and public opinion, and Christians have essential technical skills or occupy positions of authority that give them opportunities to shape the outcomes. Although Bonhoeffer wanted to treat ventures of responsibility as extraordinary events, the task and the opportunity to remake society in responsible cooperation with others have been very much with us in the years since World War II. These tasks and opportunities link our own less dramatic experience to the moral guidance that Bonhoeffer offered to the *Abwehr* conspirators as he formulated the system of his *Ethics*. Whatever Bonhoeffer intended, his advice is for us, too, when the ordinary rules of morality fail us and we must renew the possibilities for moral action. On these occasions, the Christian acts, not out of self-interest, but to protect those who otherwise would suffer. To risk guilt is hardly remarkable if it means only that we will sacrifice our integrity to protect our own skins. People do that all the time. What characterizes responsible action is "deputyship," standing in on behalf of those who are powerless to act for themselves and using what power we have for their protection.[49] Responsibility can have dramatic consequences in the central events of history, but it is rare enough in any circumstances, and when it is exercised on the smaller scale of city politics, business decisions, family choices, and congregational meetings, it upsets the predictable patterns of self-interested behavior and creates unexpected opportunities to introduce new forms of cooperation. In these ways, too, those who "live by responding to the word of God which is addressed to us in Jesus Christ"[50] take history into their hands.

A Public Venture?

The central importance of responsiveness to Christ in Bonhoeffer's venture of responsibility is something of a puzzle for understanding his own ventures. Clearly, the *Abwehr* conspiracy was not a theology seminar, and Bonhoeffer, as he moved more closely into its workings, also moved away from the distinctly ecclesiastical identity he had maintained since 1933. How far then did he think that his understanding of his actions could be shared by all the others who engaged in action with him? We have seen how Bonhoeffer's venture was Christian. We must now ask whether it can also be ethics in the ordinary, public sense.

Certainly the venture of responsibility requires cooperative action. Strategies and the immediate goals of action must be understood by everyone involved, or else the venturers will find themselves working at cross-purposes in ways that will quickly destroy the plan if not the participants. Yet Christians enter the venture with the intention to reestablish obedience to God, an aim which those who act along with them may neither understand nor endorse. Bonhoeffer thinks that a Christian who believes in God's power to forgive and does not treat human righteousness as an end in itself is more likely to summon the courage to act responsibly than one whose final point of reference is personal integrity or the sanctity of an oath, but is this Christian courage simply an affirmation of choices that everyone might make on purely practical grounds, or does Bonhoeffer think that the Christian is likely to choose differently from others because of his or her faith?

What is most clearly public in the venture of responsibility is the action. It is public not in the way that the Confessing Church's symbolic resistance was public because it was always conducted openly. (Indeed, some part of most ventures of responsibility must remain closely held secrets.) Rather, responsible action is public in the sense that what is done should be understandable to persons generally, and because the public is expected to understand what is happening, they are also expected to respond to it. The twentieth of July conspirators did not expect that their action would be universally accepted, but they did expect everyone to understand the meaning of their removal of Hitler and their takeover of the government. They expected, too, that those who were affected would respond in the light of this meaning. They saw their conspiracy as a moral act which would demand subsequent actions from others, not by force, but as a matter of right. The German people were to recognize the coup d'état as the restoration of government by law, and they were to accord the new government the obedience that law demands, whatever their feelings had been about Hitler. The Allied powers at war with Germany were to recognize this as a renunciation of the aggressive lawlessness that had brought the world to war, and they were to offer the new government peace terms quite different from those they would have imposed on the Nazis.

Characteristically, the appeals for understanding that accompany responsible action are a mixture of moral and nonmoral arguments.

An act of religious witness may proclaim quite openly, "Here I stand," on the basis of its hearing of the Word of God. A public argument that seeks first to secure agreement on a course of action recognizes that people have many reasons for supporting an action, and it appeals to as many of these motives as possible. Both the German people and the Allies might welcome a new regime that promised to cut short the danger and destruction of war. In time the Allies might have offered more generous peace terms for the very practical reason that the punitive arrangements imposed on Germany in 1919 had never worked. A venture of responsibility must itself be selfless, but that does not preclude appeals to others based on their self-interested concerns as well as appeals to moral understanding.

Nevertheless, the moral appeal is also clearly present. When Bonhoeffer insists that "No attempt can succeed which aims at saving the west while excluding one of the western nations,"[51] he is not saying that the Allies lack the power to impose a punitive and exclusionary settlement on Germany. He is appealing for moral awareness.

> [At] this point, even within the history of the internal and external political struggle of the nations, there is something in the nature of forgiveness, though it be only a faint shadow of the forgiveness which Jesus Christ vouchsafes to faith. What happens here is the waiving of the demand that the guilty man shall fully expiate the wrong he has committed. . . . Not all the wounds inflicted can be healed, but what matters is that there shall be no further wounds.[52]

Bonhoeffer would remind the victors that the institutions of Western society cannot perform their moral functions while any nation or institution is crushed by the burden of requirements to repair what cannot in fact be undone. The call for "something in the nature of forgiveness" within and between the nations of Europe aims to enlist people and leaders in a venture of responsibility in ending the war on terms that will allow the reemergence of a just and ordered society in all of the nations involved. Bonhoeffer lays that claim on the statesmen of Europe in the *Ethics,* as clearly as he tried to convey it to the British government in his clandestine meetings with Bishop Bell in Sweden. The moral implications of the conspirators' proposal should have been clear, at least to anyone whose thinking about politics had been formed in the Western context. No special theological interpretation is required to understand the appropriate response to the changes in Germany's government which the twentieth of July conspirators proposed. Their venture of responsibility was clear in itself, and the claim it made on the actions of the Allies was equally apparent. The diplomatic mission which Bonhoeffer undertook as agent for the *Abwehr* and courier for the conspiracy needed no further explanation.

Nevertheless, Bonhoeffer the theologian felt compelled to add something more. That "something in the nature of forgiveness" which is a part of Western ethics and Western politics is "only a faint shadow of the forgiveness which Jesus Christ vouchsafes to faith." Political forgiveness, giving up the demand that the guilty party must restore everything just as it was before, provides a useful guideline for responsible action to reestablish relationships after a political conflict. What political forgiveness cannot comprehend, however, is the theological forgiveness that does not concern itself with degrees of guilt, but condemns all faults utterly (including the faults of the responsible parties who overstep their limits while working to end the era of disobedience) in order that all may be totally forgiven.

Bonhoeffer thus introduces a distinction into his venture of action between a fully Christian theological understanding of events and a political understanding which guides responsible action. The Christian may very well participate in the political action, and it is quite appropriate to describe that action as righteous in ordinary moral terms. Righteous action, action that allows the institutions of society to function in ways that acknowledge our multiple obligations and that allows us to respond in obedience, is important, and Christians must be able to choose and to do the things that make for righteousness. What they must never forget, however is just what this public, political process with its choices and decisions can never comprehend: rightious actions in no way makers a righteous actor. The justified moral decision does not justify the decision maker. Instead, all who act decisively—the Christian who respects the structure of the divine mandates no less than the "successful man" who shatters them—incur guilt and have their hope for justification only in forgiveness. Action which takes place in a search for self-justification or in a self-confidence based on a superior righteousness, therefore, cannot be fully Christian obedience. Obedience occurs only when self-seeking is abandoned in the mystery of atonement and the search for righteousness is given up in acceptance of reconciliation. The ventures we undertake are never a goal in themselves. They are at most an act of grateful acknowledgement of God's goals, a recognition that Christ is taking form in our history and continues reconciling the world to himself despite our efforts and never because of them.

Christians must therefore maintain a "secret discipline" (*Arcandiszip-*

lin) among themselves.[53] By this Bonhoeffer does not mean some private truths reserved only for the initiated but simply a discipline of study, worship, and discourse in which the basic concepts of traditional theology—"concepts of repentance, faith, justification, rebirth, and sanctification"—can retain the fullness of meaning they have largely lost in the world of action. Bonhoeffer had no desire to keep these theological truths a secret. Indeed, reinterpreting them in a secular sense was an important part of the work he hoped to do after the war.[54] In the meantime, however, the demands of righteous action in the ordinary sense of 'righteous' could not be delayed, even though the distinction between that righteousness and Christian obedience could not be denied.

Bonhoeffer's ethical system, then, is clearly more public than Barth's. Barth could not acknowledge a righteous action distinct from obedience which would have any moral significance for Christians. His repeated insistence, in dialectical and analogical styles, that true Christian action consists only in an obedience which cannot be identified by any public signs appears again in his evaluation of Bonhoeffer's crucial venture of responsibility. When Barth comes to assess the attempt on Hitler's life, he acknowledges the Christian tradition that permits tyrannicide in the extreme cases, where there is no other recourse to end the dictator's destruction and brutality. Evaluating the twentieth of July plot, however, could not for Barth be a matter of applying that general principle to this particular case. The crucial question is whether this act of tyrannicide would be an act of obedience to God, not whether it conforms to a general rule. Barth concludes from the fact that the conspirators failed to carry out their plan that they must have at least had doubts about it. "The plan miscarried simply because no one was prepared to go through with it in absolute disregard of his own life. . . . The only lesson to be learned is that they had no clear and categorical command from God to do it." On the other hand, Barth will not elevate the fact of failure in this case to a divine veto on tyrannicide. We cannot "seriously blame these men for seriously considering and even deciding upon assassination. In such a situation, it might well have been the command of God. For all we know, perhaps it was, and they failed to hear it."[55] Where the question is one of obedience in a specific situation, there is simply no way to tell. To the earlier list of Christian possibilities—"these principles of his may be conservative or revolutionary: he may be . . . a Pietist, perhaps, but quite as well a Communist"[56]—we must now add: "He may be an assassin, or he may not!"

Bonhoeffer will not leave the question of action in such a state of obscurity. Of course, there can be no question of an ultimate theological justification of tyrannicide. The guilt of the conspirators remains, for all the good they might have done and intended to do. Tyrannicide, however, can be an essential element in a more comprehensive plan to restore the state to its proper function in society. Where assassination is undertaken for dramatic effect, or for crude vengeance, or merely as a power play to replace one dictator with another it is wrong. As a part of a venture of responsibility, however, it may be an unavoidable necessity. Bonhoeffer understood those Christians who shrank from the deed, and he did not think in terms of a general moral *duty* to kill tyrants. The responsibility, as always, is a matter of task and opportunity; but when the task and the opportunity presented themselves, Bonhoeffer could not avoid asking whether this act might be necessary for the restoration of order in European society. That discussion and decision was a closely guarded secret, but it was also, in an important way, a public moral choice. The conspiracy was responsible precisely because its desperate choice could be understood by anyone who had lived under the Nazi regime and knew the impossibility of ordinary moral action in the face of the government's demand for total loyalty and unlimited obedience.

On the other hand, Bonhoeffer's responsible action is clearly less public than the responsiveness to the orders of creation described by Emil Brunner. If Barth takes no theological interest in moral righteousness that is different from simple obedience to the Word of God, Brunner insists that a righteousness responsible to the orders of creation can be understood theologically as a form of obedience to God. Bonhoeffer struck a position between them, preserving the Barthian distinction between moral righteousness and Christian obedience, but, like Brunner, giving moral righteousness a foundation in reality and a theological significance.

The principal difference between Bonhoeffer's mandates and Brunner's orders is that Bonhoeffer incorporates into the mandates an element of theology and history that cannot be understood in purely natural terms. Brunner argues that the orders of creation are shaped by invariant requirements that apply in all ages. For Bonhoeffer, the requirements that govern labor, marriage, church, or state are not absolutes built into nature but limits that have evolved in history. He is primarily interested in the form these limits take in the West, where the influence of biblical norms and the continuing reality of the church exert powerful forces on all social institutions. The historical development of the mandates in the West can, of course, be discerned by any thoughtful observer, but unless one's conception of the social reality under study includes the formative presence of Christ, some of the coherence and intelligibility of that history will be lost. The 'natural' is a limiting concept, not an exhaustive explanation. In the Protestant "rediscovery of the natural,"[57] what we rediscover is primarily that there *are* limits. The power of human thought to reshape life and culture is not so great as either Hitler or the Hegelians have imagined. Just what those limits are, however, appears more clearly in history and theology than in nature alone. Certainly the requirements cannot be settled by a direct appeal to natural law or natural right.

The actual source of limits for Bonhoeffer is the power of God to shape history and the continual formation and reformation of human life in Jesus Christ. This can never be understood by those who deny the reality of Christ or try to make it into a system of sociological laws or rules of reason. At the same time—just because this formative power is a reality—thoughtful persons who recognize the limits that reality imposes on every human enterprise will often be in agreement with Christians on just what responsible actions are demanded by formation and reformation. Indeed, the intelligent, expert non-Christian may perhaps even be ahead of the church in the skills and opportunities necessary to implement a responsible plan. Righteous action may leave more scope for human pride than simple Christian obedience, and it may not have so clear a view of its own limitations, but the obedient Christian cannot stand aloof from it.[58]

Moreover, the evidence of Bonhoeffer's later writings is that he did not think this distance in understanding was too great to be bridged. For Barth, the difference between moral action and obedience is important in principle and must always be retained as a witness against the pretensions of human morality. Bonhoeffer, perhaps, thought toward the end of his life that this was a temporary problem. The conceptual distinction is important, of course, but it has been magnified by the church's failure to speak its formative word clearly, and by the West's hostility to Christ which has shaped so much of recent history.

The secret of the Christian's secret discipline then is not an incomprehensible truth to be guarded from profane ears but a testimony to the church's failure to speak of a reality that includes Christ in ways that others who respect reality could understand.

> Reconciliation and redemption, regeneration and the Holy Spirit, love of our enemies, cross and resurrection, life in Christ and Christian discipleship—all these things are so difficult and so remote that we hardly

venture any more to speak of them. In the traditional words and acts, we suspect that there may be something quite new and revolutionary, though we cannot as yet grasp or express it. That is our own fault. Our church, which has been fighting in these years only for its own self-preservation, as though that were an end in itself, is incapable of taking the word of reconciliation and redemption to mankind and the world. Our earlier words are therefore bound to lose their force and cease, and our being Christian today will be limited to two things: prayer and righteous action among men. All Christian thinking, speaking, and organizing must be born anew out of this prayer and action. . . . It is not for us to prophesy the day (though the day will come) when men will once more be called so to utter the word of God that the world will be changed and renewed by it. It will be a new language, perhaps quite non-religious, but liberating and redeeming, as was Jesus' language; it will shock people and overcome them by its power; it will be the language of a new righteousness and truth, proclaiming God's peace with men and the coming of his kingdom.[59]

It is clear, then, that the purpose of the "non-religious" interpretation of Christianity is not to purge it of the elements that distinguish it from secular wisdom but precisely to communicate Christianity's distinctive apprehension of Western history and institutions—and so of reality itself—to all. Successful communication here would not end the need for public moral decisions. Occasions for responsible action would still arise, but the Christian understanding would increasingly be a persuasive understanding of reality on which all parties to the discussion could agree. The distance between fully obedient action which lets Christ take form in our history and the righteous action that displays prudent respect for the "natural" limits on our lives would be correspondingly reduced.

These suggestive passages in Bonhoeffer's prison writings parallel developments in Roman Catholic moral theology. Recent writers on natural law complain that the standard scholastic approach to the subject, with its hierarchy of natural ends known by reason neatly subordinated to spiritual ends known by faith, conveys the impression that a complete description of human life in natural terms could simply ignore the reality of human alienation from God and the mystery of redemption. Our relationship to God, these writers argue, must be the fundamental reality that pervades and somehow shapes even our "natural" humanity.[60] The assumption of earlier natural law theorists that reason alone will tell us everything we need to know about human nature gives way to a recognition that human nature itself is involved in the history of salvation. Nevertheless, these writers have no desire to transform the natural law into a private morality claimed by Christians alone. Their aim is to make the implications of grace rationally comprehensible to all, Christians and non-Christians alike.

> In practice, it is irrelevant to ask whether there are commandments or prohibitions . . . which only the Christian can know on the basis of faith and which are therefore only obligatory for him. For us, it is less interesting to ask whether the moral norms of Christianity are originally and exclusively Christian than whether or not they can be communicated. I am of the opinion that it must be possible to communicate to all men the consequences for human relationships that result from our faith in God and his liberating love.[61]

If the suggestions in Bonhoeffer's prison writings are followed out, it appears that he moved closer to this Roman Catholic view of natural law which is rooted in moral theology, just as Brunner moved closer to a Catholic natural law which relies more heavily on rational moral philosophy.[62] In both cases, the Protestant authors seemed to learn from the experiences of totalitarianism, war, and resistance a new respect for the efforts to formulate in general terms what human nature requires for its fulfillment and the moral demands that these requirements impose on all persons and governments. Brunner stresses the discernment of these requirements in a law of nature which all persons suffering under misrule can know and invoke. Bonhoeffer stresses communication in terms that all can understand of requirements that are apprehended with unique insight in the community that sees Christ taking form in history. What separates Bonhoeffer from contemporary Roman Catholics like Franz Böckle and Josef Fuchs is not his final assessment of the task of moral theology but the fact that he is less optimistic about our ability to communicate its insights to a culture which does not share in the revelation of faith and often seems actively hostile to what it does discern of it. Communicating to all the "consequences for human relationships that result from our faith in God and his liberating love" may have to wait for a time for which we can only hope. Meanwhile, Bonhoeffer would not have us neglect the demands of righteous action.

NOTES

1. Dietrich Bonhoeffer, *Creation and Fall; Temptation: Two Biblical Studies* (New York: Macmillan Co., 1959), 88.

2. References to Bonhoeffer's *Ethics* are to the English translation based on the arrangement of the sixth German edition. The chapters have been arranged in the order that they were written.

3. Bonhoeffer, *Ethics*, 40.

4. Brunner, *The Divine Imperative*, 56.

5. Bonhoeffer's thought and teaching from 1934 to 1937 can be studied in two works which began in the seminary at Finkenwalde, *The Cost of Discipleship*, and *Life Together* (New York: Harper & Row, 1954). The first section of *Ethics*, "The Love of God and the Decay of the World," 17–54, reflects the thinking of that period as well.

6. Bonhoeffer, *Cost of Discipleship*, 223.

7. Quoted in Cochrane, *The Church's Confession*, 40.

8. Karl Barth, in a letter of June 25, 1935, quoted in Eberhard Bethge, *Dietrich Bonhoeffer* (New York: Harper & Row, 1970), 354.

9. Helmreich, *German Churches*, 227–29.

10. Bethge, *Bonhoeffer*, 661–74.

11. Bonhoeffer's *Letters and Papers* was written largely during his imprisonment in Berlin's Tegel military prison following his arrest.

12. Thielicke, *Theological Ethics* (Philadelphia: Fortress Press, 1969), 2: 401.

13. Dietrich Bonhoeffer, *No Rusty Swords*, ed. E. H. Robertson (London: William Collins & Sons, 1970), 77.

14. Bonhoeffer, *Ethics*, 207. Bonhoeffer's list of mandates varies slightly in different chapters of the *Ethics*, but the church, labor, marriage and the family, the state or government, and culture are all mentioned in one place or another.

15. Ibid., 143.

16. Ibid., 88–89.

17. Ibid., 108.

18. Ibid. Bonhoeffer chooses the term 'formation' as a deliberate play on the older notion of 'Christian formation', a program of education and spiritual guidance to lead persons into a life modeled on Christ. The key question, Bonhoeffer suggests, is not how we take on the form of Christ but how Christ takes form among us.

19. Bonhoeffer, *Ethics*, 88.

20. Ibid., 279.

21. Ibid., 263.

22. Ibid., 287.

23. Ibid., 274.

24. Ibid., 114.

25. Ibid., 115.

26. Ibid., 108–109.

27. Ibid., 75–76.

28. Ibid., 343.

29. Bethge, *Bonhoeffer*, 525.

30. *Germans Against Hitler: July 20, 1944* (Bonn: Press and Information Office of the Federal Republic of Germany, 1969), 166.

31. S. William Halperin, *Germany Tried Democracy* (New York: W. W. Norton, 1965), 430ff.

32. *Germans Against Hitler*, 163.

33. Bethge, *Bonhoeffer*, 834.

34. Bonhoeffer, *Letters and Papers* 16. Bonhoeffer wrote these lines in an essay which he gave to several associates in the conspiracy some weeks before his arrest.

35. Bonhoeffer, *Letters and Papers,* 6.

36. Bonhoeffer, *Ethics,* 97–98.

37. Ibid., 269.

38. Ibid., 222.

39. Ibid.

40. Ibid.

41. Bonhoeffer's venture of responsibility thus differs from the concept of human responsibility in H. Richard Neibuhr's important study, *The Responsible Self* (New York: Harper & Row, 1963). For Niebuhr responsibility, in the sense of responsiveness to our encounters with other persons and with God, is the criterion of Christian moral action in *every* situation. It is our responsiveness to the interaction of our actions with the consciousness of others, Niebuhr suggests, that distinguishes Christian ethics from the rigidities of deontology and the tendency of teleology to reduce persons to mere means to an end. Bonhoeffer would agree, of course, with the rejection of abstract ethical systems, but he would doubtless find Niebuhr's concept of responsibility of much broader application than his own idea of *Verantwortung*.

42. Bonhoeffer, *Ethics,* 315.

43. Bonhoeffer, *Letters and Papers,* 10–11.

44. Ibid., 44.

45. See chapter 3, 57.

46. Barth, *Church Dogmatics,* 3/4, 22.

47. Bonhoeffer, *Ethics,* 239.

48. For a critical study of the aristocratic presuppositions of the leaders of the *Abwehr* conspiracy, see Larry Rasmussen, *Dietrich Bonhoeffer: Reality and Resistance* (Nashville: Abingdon Press, 1972).

49. Bonhoeffer, *Ethics,* 224–27.

50. Ibid., 222.

51. Ibid., 119.

52. Ibid., 118.

53. Bonhoeffer, *Letters and Papers,* 268.

54. Much has been made of Bonhoeffer's letters about "religionless Christianity." (See *Letters and Papers,* 278–81.) Because a brief collection of his prison letters became known in English before the rest of his work, American interpreters were able to read into Bonhoeffer's suggestive fragments their own concern for a Christianity that would do without God or at least without language about God. (See Langdon Gilkey, *Naming the Whirlwind: The Renewal of God Language* [Indianapolis: Bobbs-Merrill, 1969], 108–9.) Whatever the merits of that idea, it seems clear that Bonhoeffer's own intention was to continue Barth's effort to purge Christianity of a "religious" element that gives Christians a false sense of security and encourages self-righteous actions. Bonhoeffer's own contribution was to insist that a "religionless Christianity," which will be precisely a Christianity that depends solely on God, must not at the same time become a "revelational positivism."

55. Barth, *Church Dogmatics,* 3/4, 449.

56. Idem, *The Holy Ghost,* 81.

57. Bonhoeffer, *Ethics,* 143–49; *Letters and Papers,* 10.

58. See Albert R. Jønsen, *Responsibility in Modern Religious Ethics*

(Washington D.C.,: Corpus Books, 1968), 121–28.

59. Bonhoeffer, *Letters and Papers,* 299–300.

60. See Fuchs, *Natural Law,* 42–52; also see the discussions of recent litera-ture in Richard McCormick, *Notes on Moral Theology: 1965–1980* (Washington, D.C.: University Press of America, 1981), 130–37; 626–36.

61. Franz Böckle, *Fundamental Moral Theology,* trans. N. D. Smith (New York: Pueblo Publishing Company, 1980), 180.

62. See chapter 4, 97.

7
FAITH
FOR A NEW PATH

Karl Barth, Emil Brunner, and Dietrich Bonhoeffer—these three theologians lived and wrote in one of the most intense periods of change in Western history. From the collapse of the European empires and the ensuing confusion through the rise and ruin of fascist certainty to the emergence of the communist Soviet Union as a major power, a little less than thirty years elapsed. The theologians tried to understand this kaleidoscope of issues, but they worked with the conviction that the fundamental problems were matters of theology, not of policy. So we do not have from them extended essays on totalitarianism and social justice or on the ethics of propaganda and the police state. We do not have such treatises, not only because it would have been unsafe to write them. For these authors, it was more important to delineate the basic structure of the Christian moral life than to analyze particular policies.

What they sought, then, were constraints on action that do not change through the wild swings of the political pendulum. Brunner sought *orders of creation* that endure across times and cultures. Bonhoeffer speaks of *divine mandates,* and Barth eventually returns to general guides for action in the *prominent lines* of Jesus' teaching about discipleship. In indicating what these interpretive systems required in action, each author tried to speak in terms appropriate to the whole history of Western Christianity, if not the whole of human culture.

The scope of these statements serves another purpose as well. To speak in terms of major social systems or persistent patterns of action opens the way for ethical specificity. Barth, Brunner, and Bonhoeffer share a traditional Christian wariness of legalism in morals, but they express this suspicion in an especially vigorous rejection of *universal* moral principles of the Kantian sort, rules which claim to provide tests of conduct appropriate to all human beings without regard for individual peculiarities or for the distinctiveness of their historical situations. To escape this rationalized universalism, which for them vitiated philosophical ethics, the theologians were obliged either to forego specific guidance altogether or to give that guidance in the form of a suggestion about where valid moral insights might be found. Each in his own way identifies forms of human activity in which the Word of God can be heard and followed, in contrast to other activities that merely express our heedlessness or willful rejection of God's purposes. So without specifying in advance what the outcome of the exploration must be, Brunner directs us to "critical cooperation" with the material and social imperatives of the orders; Bonhoeffer stresses the legitimate structures of command and obedience that characterize each of the divine mandates; and Barth calls us to the community of faith which reflects on the persistent demands of discipleship.

All of this not only rejects the philosophical method of ethical generalization, it also contrasts sharply with the theological thinking about ethics that prevailed before World War I. Despite some complaints against the industrial system by religious socialists, the religious mood of that time was one of satisfaction with the prevailing order of things. Christianity looked forward, not back. Instead of seeking a critical perspective on the present time in Scripture and the traditions of the church, theologians turned a critical eye to the Scripture itself and found in the movements of their own day the measure of all things. The appearance, in the midst of postwar disillusionment, of an existentialist orientation that detected widespread evidence of cultural decay seemed a dramatic shift at the time, but as Barth later realized, it marked no essential change. The prevailing mood, whether of optimism or despair, carried everything before it, and few considered that Christianity might represent a fundamentally different perspective on events.

The theological movement which Barth, Brunner, and others began in Switzerland rejected from the outset this assimilation of Christianity into the culture. Christian action begins, Barth insisted, not in some widely shared consensus on the meaning of events, but in simple obedience to the Word of God. That fundamental idea returns, not only in Brunner and Bonhoeffer, but in a host of other Protestant writers of the time and of the years that followed. Christian ethics is a matter of responsiveness to the commands of God, who remains free and active in history. God's freedom cannot be captured in a formula or reduced to a set of rules. The theologians might argue, as many philosphers have done before and since, that general moral rules always fail in particular situations. What distinguished the theological critique, however, was the underlying contrast between a generalization which arises out of the human situation and a Word which is addressed to it from the outside.

Barth, Brunner, and Bonhoeffer all insisted on this distinction between their ethical thought and all other systems, philosophical or theological, which take the "point of contact" between the prevailing culture and Christian faith for granted. Their unanimity on this point should not, however, obscure for us the very real differences between them over the special problems which an ethics of obedience raises.

Brunner and Bonhoeffer envision an obedience which can be lived out in partnership with others who do not share the Christian faith. Acts which for Christians have a special significance as obedience to the commands of God nevertheless make sense in terms of material and social requirements (orders of creation) or hierarchies of command and obedience (mandates) which everyone can understand. The Christian ethic is more than, but not other than, the functional requirements of a society in which human life can flourish. So understood, Brunner and Bonhoeffer converge with the main currents of modern Catholic thought on natural law.

Barth, however, remains alone, isolated but not insignificant. If we can no longer simply equate cultural norms and Christian obedience, he also insists that we can never presume even the general outlines of a reconciliation between them.

The authors we have examined, then, all point us to the problem of living Christian faith in ambiguous situations, without the guidance of general rules and, above all, without the presumption that a life in harmony with the culture will also meet the requirements of discipleship. They do not agree on the solution to this problem, but they do hold it before us. Their clarity may keep us from losing the path in the thicket of issues that demand our attention, and the alternatives that they offered for European Protestant Christianity toward the beginning of the twentieth century may help us to sort out our choices in the wider ecumenical world in which we now live.

The Obedient Community

Those who follow Barth will seek guidance in a community of faith that understands the world in faith's own terms and is indifferent to the meanings things have in the world. This community may be a gathered

Christian congregation in some traditional form, or it may be a community joined together in intentional commitment for an exploration of the faith. In either case, the community will give significant attention to the marks that identify it as a locus of discipleship and distinguish it from other groups which serve the identifiable social functions of education, public order, and economic productivity. The aim of ethics in this theology is, as Stanley Hauerwas puts it, "to reassert the significance of the church as a distinct society with an integrity peculiar to itself."[1] The community of faith must not be confused with these institutions, must not become another order or mandate alongside them. The lines of discipleship lead in their own directions, and often as not these will run opposite to what the world requires to maintain order, achieve prosperity, and secure happiness.

Such communities of faith can perhaps see the world's corruption with clearer sight than those whose activities are closely tied to the culture. Theologians in Latin America today often envision a church in which the most important units would be "base communities," rather than conventional parishes. They argue that the only way to break the grip of traditional, oligarchical social patterns which pervade even the churches is to bring people together for Bible study and sacramental sharing in groups that defy existing social distinctions and offer an alternative to the values that now prevail. So, too, the historic "peace churches" in the United States have maintained a constant witness against military activity, unaffected by the ebb and flow of public sentiment in the wider society. More recently, the churches of North America and Western Europe have been urged to become centers of resistance to "consumerism." As awareness of global shortages of food and resources grows, some persons seek alternatives to the economic patterns which they believe are largely responsible for the problems, and they find a starting point in a community of faith that will resist the cultural emphasis on acquiring more and more possessions.[2] The Christian rejection of consumerism is reminiscent of Barth's 1958 warning to the pastors and people of East Germany that Western prosperity and freedom are not sufficient theological reasons to desire reunification with the West.[3]

For all the communities, the life of Christian faith begins with a rejection of the pretensions to virtue that political and cultural systems make. When corporations advertise the prosperity that their enterprises create and governments present themselves as defenders of freedom, these communities of faith regard their claims with suspicion.

Indeed, they usually regard global politics as an arena of mere power, in which ideological systems vie for loyalty and maintain their hold on the populace by systematic deceptions calculated to provoke fear of rival systems.

This general condemnation of existing political systems reinforces the idea that genuine moral relationships are possible only within the community of faith. It leaves little scope for the traditional categories of international political morality—the concepts of legitimate government, the law of nations, and the principles of national sovereignty and self-determination. Indeed, the contemporary communities of faith usually follow Barth in rejecting all attempts to formulate moral principles that could provide a constant standard against which to judge particular historic institutions. They regard the idea of natural law as misleadingly unspecific and unchanging. These suspicions prevail even among Roman Catholic theologians who are, as a matter of doctrine, committed to retain some concept of natural law in their moral theology. A natural law based on Christian discipleship rather than on a rational assessment of human purposes provides the basis for moral theology in the community of faith.

> In a more metaphysical idiom the being or *esse* of the Christian from which his behavior or action is to flow (*actio sequitur esse*) is the human being transformed by participation in divine sonship. Traditional natural law understanding of morality must be reconsidered in the setting of the redemptive transformation involved for mankind as sons of the Father.[4]

Here the natural law tension between a universal norm and a concrete situation is replaced by an eschatological tension between humanity transformed by God and the present human condition, and this tension is heightened by the experience of the beginnings of that transformation through membership in the Christian community. This sense of participation in the uncompleted but nonetheless present work of God, this "already/not yet" experience of salvation, provides the vantage point from which many contemporary Christian communities view their own place in history. This modification of traditional moral theology is reinforced, moreover, by contemporary biblical scholarship, which finds in the early Christian communities who gave us the New Testament an atmosphere of eschatological expectation which subsequent ages in theology often failed to understand. Those who approach the questions of New Testament ethics today have obtained from the biblical scholars "a greater capacity to conceive the meaning of scriptural thought within its own original cultural context, a capacity for cultural empathy probably greater than has obtained at any time since the end of the Apostolic Age."[5] Thus despite the long emphasis in moral theology on norms grounded in unchanging nature, ethicists who stress the transformation of nature by Christ do so with some confidence that they have recovered the understanding of the redemptive event which was also the understanding of the early church.

Thus prepared with theological and biblical arguments to modify traditional moral theology, ethicists who stress the importance of communities of faith usually also continue Barth's indictment of moral philosophy.

> At least partly under the inspiration of the scientific ideal of objectivity, contemporary ethical theory has tried to secure for moral judgments an objectivity that would free such judgments from the subjective beliefs, wants, and stories of the agent who makes them. Just as science thus tries to insure objectivity by adhering to an explicitly disinterested method, so ethical theory tried to show that moral judgments, insofar as they can be considered true, must be the result of an impersonal rationality.[6]

The problem with this "standard account of moral rationality," Stanley Hauerwas suggests, is that the interests which define an agent as a person and the beliefs and narratives that link the agent to a community of faith are crucial elements that make choices meaningful for real persons in concrete situations. An ethical theory that is rational or "objective" in these scientific terms may define a moral dilemma precisely, but it cannot tell a real person what it is appropriate to do in the situation.

Today, the theological critics of ethical theory have closer allies among the philosophers than Barth found in his own time. We noted in Barth's treatment of moral issues certain comparisons with existentialist and positivist philosophers who were also critical of a universalized moral rationality. Barth's affinity with the existentialists and positivists, however, was largely on points of attack against Kantian ethics and the subsequent tradition of German idealism. Barth's ethics as he understands it has little in common with either the existentialists' despair or the positivists' ethical relativism. By contrast, many present-day critics of rules and principles in moral philosophy agree with their theological counterparts on the program for a more adequate ethics. This would include a recognition of the particular character of each moral agent and a recovery of the concepts of virtue by which communities of faith and identity shape the moral perceptions of their members.[7]

The principal distinction between Barth and these contemporary successors lies in his stress on the specific demands of obedience in each situation, which contrasts with the contemporary emphasis on a general orientation toward events which the community of faith derives from its "already/not yet" perspective on history. That perspective is clearly not foreign to Barth. He insists for example that the certainty of conscience is "already" a knowing-with-God, but he also argues that we have this certainty "only eschatologically." It is "not yet" fully in our possession.[8] For Barth, this eschatological expectation serves primarily as a warning not to generalize about the demands of obedience but to listen always for the specific command of God. For at least some contemporary theologians, the "already/not yet" perspective is a warrant for a certain set of expectations about moral life and the results of human action generally. On the one hand, the "already/not yet" may be taken to imply the impossibility of any significant change within the life of society. The demands of faith must be lived out in the community of faith, where a new reality has already begun to be realized, but it would be a serious mistake to suppose that these demands could find much fulfillment in a wider society which has so far not even grasped its own situation in relation to the judgment of God.[9] On the other hand, the "already/not yet" may become a warrant for the most radical social change. Since the existing reality is so clearly without a moral foundation and rests on sytematic distortions, the only way to establish relations between persons that could meet the demands of faith is to discard the existing social framework and replace it with something totally new. From this point of view, the revolutionary implications of Christianity lie not alone in its ability to form a community that is free of the deceptions of culture but also in its vision of a wider society organized without oppression.[10]

What these quite different approaches have in common that links them to the ethics of Karl Barth, and especially to Barth's early work, is the conviction that nothing is accomplished by working within the framework of society and outside the community of the faith. There is here no "critical cooperation" with the orders of creation, no "venture of responsibility" that reestablishes the conditions for obedience within the social framework inherited from our Western, Christian past. Discipleship follows its own imperatives, which are not related to the foundational requirements of existing societies. Any trace of divine intention in our human heritage has been obliterated by the distortions which conceal the true workings of power in society and which make it all but impossible to communicate directly any intentions, human or

165

divine. Attempts to correct the flaws of the existing order are not only unlikely to succeed; they expose one to the dangerous illusion that what happens in society actually has some ultimate significance. From the point of view of a community of faith which finds meaning chiefly in the relationships that exist within it, the errors of liberal Protestantism against which Barth first raised objections are merely an extreme form of a confusion which has prevailed in the church in all ages. Those whose work and hopes are tied to the secular order are obliged to take it seriously on its own terms. If they are also Christians, it is almost inevitable that they will confuse that seriousness with the demands that spring from faith. What are merely limitations and requirements of conditioned human activity begin to assume the unconditioned importance of the command of God.

It is of utmost importance, then, that the church preserve its freedom from the surrounding culture. This need not imply a withdrawing strategy that refuses to take any active role in the life of society. Whether or not such an attitude ever prevailed in sectarian Protestant communities, it clearly does not dominate the active social witness of those churches in peace, disaster relief, and food programs today. Nor does withdrawal characterize the "base communities" of liberation theology. Freedom is marked, rather, by a careful, continuous scrutiny of activity to avoid being caught up in the quest for success and the manipulation of power that often mark ordinary human activity. What the church does or refrains from doing is marked, rather, by dependence on the initiative of God. "The church does not attack the powers; this Christ has done. The church concentrates on not being seduced by them. By her existence she demonstrates that their rebellion has been vanquished."[11]

The church, then, may resist obvious evil, but it will be equally concerned to keep its distance from apparent good. What links the Christian groups who struggle with repressive governments in Asia or Latin America to their counterparts in the less hostile environment of North America or Western Europe is the conviction that the church must keep its distance from those who would support it for their own purposes, just as the church must be ready to suffer at the hands of those who cannot tolerate its freedom. That is the attitude which many Christians have learned in experience rather than in theology. Not all of those who hold it today know that it was articulated half a century ago by Karl Barth for the Confessing Church in Hitler's Germany; but whenever a group seeks a theological foundation for its suspicions about the surrounding culture, it eventually rediscovers the terms in which Barth shattered the synthesis of faith and culture. The Word of God is a word of command beyond our knowledge or control. It directs us into paths that cannot be guessed from historical developments or guided by attentiveness to social systems. No one can command the Word of God, but those in a position to hear it are likely to be those who keep a clearer sight for the corruptions of the world and try to protect themselves from the deceptions by which the world explains itself. If they succeed in defending this freedom to be a community of obedience, they will, incidentally, secure a kind of political freedom for others as well; but that freedom is not their goal; nor are the social and legal transformations it requires the objects of their action. Political freedom is a byproduct of faithful witness to the truth; the freedom worth seeking is an obedience which expresses that witness in action.

The Commandment in the World

Attention to the concrete demands of the Word of God may, however, take another form. Brunner and Bonhoeffer, no less than Barth, rejected formal moral principles that absorb the particularities of Christian obedience into a general moral rationality, but they understood the specific problems of discipleship chiefly in terms of choices presented in historical situations. If Barth's ethical reflections ask how we can be free enough to see the difference between discipleship and the roles we have to play in the culture, Bonhoeffer and Brunner want to know how we can be disciples in situations where the roles of parent, pastor, soldier, diplomat, or worker provide the real opportunities for action that we have.

To put the matter that way demands attentiveness to the orders of creation, and indeed to those smaller subdivisions of the orders where individual lives are lived. To know what persons must do as Christians, we must first understand the real options that confront them as doctors, plant managers, or journalists, not just generally as workers; as single parents, working mothers, or absent fathers, not just generally as persons involved in marriage and family life. Those who attend to these details of life do not aim at a discipleship that remains free of the demands of social structures. They explore society's constraints carefully, for it is in knowing the real choices that are available that they can hope to identify the particular choice that would be obedient to God. An ethicist who works in this way tries to avoid becoming an uncritical apologist for an occupational group, a policy, or a social practice; but such a one also recognizes that for most of us the options for obedient action are bound up with these systems.

To be an obedient Christian in the framework of possibilities that society offers is no easy task. Indeed, as Bonhoeffer pointed out, a hostile state that respects no boundaries for its own action can render responsible action in society impossible. A church which becomes dependent on its social influence, which knows no way of working but through elaborate programs and institutions, which has to speak its message attractively in print or broadcast or becomes accustomed to whispering a word in the ear of the powerful is a church in grave danger, because it has subtly become dependent on the society in which it lives. It has lost the essential distinction on which its freedom to be the church must rest, the distinction between itself and the other orders of creation. In this sense, the church must always keep before itself the example of the Confessing Church envisioned by Karl Barth, or the church of prayer and proclamation that Bonhoeffer still desired during the worst period of Nazi repression. A church which loses this option is not free, no matter how comfortable its circumstances, while the church that keeps it remains free, even under the worst persecution.

The church must always be able to be a Confessing Church, but the church that recognizes only that possibility is also hindered in its work. It may force itself into the role of a persecuted minority when no one opposes it, simply because it knows no other way to be the church. It may neglect the real power it has to influence social life for good and at the same time self-righteously ignore the influences that society has on its own proclamation and ministry. The *status confessionis* is a challenge for Christian obedience, but the challenge that faces us most of the time is to live with the possibility of confession without retreating into it. The challenge is to participate in the life of society without losing our distinctive voice. Brunner's idea of "critical cooperation" with existing social realities and Bonhoeffer's responsible resistance mark attempts to meet this challenge. In earlier chapters, we have noted the important differences between Brunner and Bonhoeffer and considered the limitations of each of their positions. Our task now is to indicate the important points on which these authors converge to provide a basis for social ethics today.

Respect for 'The Natural'

Bonhoeffer's *Ethics* and Brunner's later work share a respect for 'the natural.'[12] If it once seemed that attentiveness to natural order could lead Christians too quickly to identify existing conditons with the will of God, the totalitarian distortions of life in Hitler's Reich indicated the importance of an awareness of limits which even powerful leaders and powerful technologies may not transgress. 'The natural' signifies persistent human needs and loyalties that cannot be set aside even to meet the demand of total war. It signifies bonds of family and local community that cannot be submerged in obedience to a distant national leader, even if parents, teachers, craftsmasters, and mayors are foolishly willing to surrender their natural authority. A state or government which recognizes those natural limits takes a positive role in protecting those more basic social units that live under its authority, but it recognizes that the central authority is not unlimited. Parliaments, cabinet ministers, and political parties do not simply decide for themselves what programs to pursue. They choose within limits laid down by natural requirements. The government that sets out to demand a political loyalty that replaces all other allegiances will eventually fail, although it may work a terrible destruction before the natural requirements overtake it. When Christians move to resist a totalitarian power, they are therefore not merely interposing their own political preferences in place of those of the regime. They act to cut short the suffering and violence that otherwise will occur, and they act to restore the conditions under which meaningful political choices can again be made. The warrant for that action, however, must be more than an immediate judgment on the present evil. It must include, as Brunner recognized during the Second World War, a conception of what nature requires of states and governments, and a conception of what nature forbids.

This respect for the natural aligns Brunner, Bonhoeffer, and their present-day successors with a wide variety of jurists and philosophers who have attempted in the last three decades to establish foundations in international law and political theory for recognized restraints on states and governments that would preclude totalitarianism and establish international standards for human rights. The language of "human rights" does not come readily to theologians who insist in the end that all human claims depend on God, but the importance of constitutional recognition that some human claims cannot be abrogated by any human authority was widely shared as European society reconstructed itself in the aftermath of Hitler's fall.[13]

The limits on state power acknowledged in constitutions and international agreements after World War II provide a framework of general moral rules for political life. They are public, not only in the sense

169

that they are embedded in public documents, but in the specific ways ethics must be public that we indicated in chapter 1; they are generalizations about action which make demands on all persons, and they are established in a public, political discourse which everyone may, in principle, enter. Yet these moral generalizations are quite different in kind from the Kantian universal laws which Brunner criticized in his early writings. Kant's moral laws were supposed to be based on reason alone and admitted no modifications from experience to qualify their relentless logical consistency. Brunner's criticism was precisely that human reason cannot achieve such perfect understanding. Sooner or later, ordinary experience contradicts the rule of reason, and we find that consistently refusing to lie would require us to betray our friends, or that always respecting the property of others would require us to stand by while landowners exploit forests and mineral deposits without regard for natural beauty or for the needs of future generations. What experience teaches us is that experience cannot be completely formulated in universal moral laws.

The limits imposed by the natural, however, are themselves learned in experience. They are like the material and social constraints Brunner recognized in the orders of creation, and their universality is a fact discovered in human history, not a requirement of logical consistency. What makes these natural limits rigorously universal is the discovery, also in human experience, that these constraints cannot be set aside by appeal to "historical necessity" or by claims that in this one instance ignoring the rights of persons and the limits on the power of the state will produce the greater good. If Protestant theologians were at one point inclined to view attempts to formulate general moral rules as expressions of human pride and an excessive confidence in reason, many of them would now acknowledge that one person's claim to be free from the constraints that bind other persons is a greater pride and a more serious threat to peace.

A new respect for the persistence of moral limits in human history thus united theologians with philosophers and jurists in an effort to delineate universal standards for personal rights, moral obligations, and limits on the power of the state, but these generalizations rested on an appeal to common human experience that was quite different from the logical consistency of Kantian moral laws. It was also different from the traditional theories of Roman Catholic natural law, at least as our Protestant theologians perceived that tradition. Influenced largely by their exposure to the manuals of moral theology written to help priests decide cases of conscience, the Protestant writers treated Catholic ethics as a deductive system imposing principles on cases by ordering human experience in inflexible, rationalistic categories.[14] What the critics overlooked and what was also somewhat obscured in the tradition itself was the way in which the first principles of moral theology were understood as statements about the human good that could be verified in anyone's experience.

The detailed investigations of social and political realities and the attentiveness to questions of policy that characterize Christian ethics today thus begins with the respect for the natural which Bonhoeffer and Brunner learned in their reflections on modern totalitarianism. Understanding the persistent features of human experience protects us from the dangerous illusion that we or our leaders can remake the human world to suit our particular designs, and it provides a standard by which to judge policy proposals and the programs of political movements. In extreme cases, as Brunner noted in *Justice and the Social Order,* these natural realities become our only point of appeal against the excesses of totalitarianism that has secured control of the sources of law and public opinion.

Understanding the persistent features of human experience is not a matter of simply repeating ancient platitudes. To understand the limits that family life, economic relationships, and faith commitments impose on political solutions, we must understand the historical, biological, and psychological forces that shape ordinary institutions. What is natural is not what is apparent or what has come to be expected. It is the limit that reality sets on our choices or on historical variation, and that boundary can be determined only in investigations that bring the power of a variety of research methods to bear on common human experience. A *Divine Imperative* written for today would doubtless incorporate more findings from the natural and social sciences in its description of the orders of creation than Brunner used in 1932, but we can already see the impetus for today's concerns with social analysis and scientific accuracy in Christian ethics in the line of argument Brunner pursued.

So the conversations with jurists, scientists, and strategists that marked Bonhoeffer's role in the conspiracy against Hitler were more than biographical footnotes. They shaped his thinking about what it meant to act responsibly, and through him, they shape our own conviction that Christian ethics must arrive at its normative conclusions in dialogue with others who share the human experience and who have their own distinctive angles of vision on it. Christian ethics conducted in this spirit refuses to give physical scientists the last word on environmental policy or to allow military strategists alone to determine defense policy, but neither does it simply interpose a conclusion drawn from Christian tradition. The demand is for an open investigation of the resources that are available to determine what actions we can take that respect the natural limits on our existence and that avoid claims to a power over our own lives we do not, in fact, possess. Sometimes this will entail support for political controls on technology that depletes irreplaceable resources or strains the capacity of fallible human beings to use it safely. Sometimes the political process itself must be restrained when a government begins to demand adjustments in the lives of families, communities, and individuals that history and our knowledge of human psychology tell us cannot be supported. At other times the resources of government, community, and economic interests must be marshaled to meet needs that would otherwise go unmet in order to prevent the distortion of human life by poverty, injustice, or disease. In all of these investigations and actions, the concerns of Christians are continuous with those of other persons in the society, and the Christian's role in public decision making is not sharply differentiated from that of others who bring their particular analytical skills and whatever traditional wisdom they possess to bear on common problems and choices. These Christians are not found in exemplary communities of witness. Indeed, they appear to be everywhere at once.

A New Christian Realism

In contrast to the radical Christianity inspired by Barth, this theological realism does not hesitate to take sides on less than ultimate issues. Barth, as we have seen repeatedly, insists that Christian faith can be identified with no side in a political conflict and that faithful Christians may as a matter of fact be found on any side. That principle was put to the test by Barth's own firm opposition to Nazism, but it emerged intact in his postwar refusal to choose on theological grounds between communism and capitalism, between East and West. A realist argues, however, that if the commitments of faith mean anything practical, they cannot evade important human choices that must be made. However difficult it may be to know with certainty what God's will or God's ordering of reality requires, we cannot avoid the attempt to discern the requirement and to make it plain to others. Realists do not expect unanimity even among Christians, but they are prepared to argue both within the church and beyond it for specific choices that are far less momentous than the issue between East and West that Barth thought faith should leave alone. Matters of arms policy and social welfare, questions of public education and criminal justice are all appropriate issues for Christian choice and therefore appropriate subjects for discussion, even within the church. If this sometimes leads church assemblies to take their deliberations too seriously and denominations to "pronounce" too solemnly, we must nevertheless recognize the serious realist point behind the resolutions: God's will and God's ordering of reality does not hover above the choices we make in society. It must be found in the details, or it will not govern in the generalities.

Avoiding both the specificity of a Barthian act-deontology and the Kantian attempt to frame moral rules that would be universally valid because they are logically necessary, the Christian realist provides the generality required for public moral discourse by expressing the basic values of the faith in terms like justice, freedom, or equality, which can be understood and argued by all, and by linking those values to relatively specific claims about what, under present conditions, must be done to realize them in society. J. H. Oldham christened these imperatives "middle axioms."[15]

> They are an attempt to define the directions in which, in a particular state of society, Christian faith must express itself. They are not binding for all time, but are provisional definitions of the type of behavior required of Christians at a given period and in given circumstances.[16]

A middle axiom seems to make a more modest claim than Brunner's delineation of the permanent, invariant orders of creation or a Thomistic account of the requirements of natural law; but the middle axiom, like these formulations, makes specific demands on the actions of persons on the basis of claims about the way the world is in reality. The Christian realist's limited appeal to the way things are in the world is nonetheless a strong claim compared with the political positivist's insistence on a consensus on action that sets aside all ultimate questions as unresolvable.[17]

Christian realism by no means abandons the traditional Protestant insistence that sin and self-centeredness distort all human thought and action. That insight is, in fact, announced as the key to a political interpretation of the contemporary world. While the idealist blithely supposes that everyone will come running to put newly proclaimed moral insights into practice, the Christian realist knows that sinful human beings will find many ways to avoid seeing the truth and to evade acting on it. Christian ethics is effective in part because it has a realistic "disposition to take all factors in a social and political situation, which offer resistance to established norms, into account."[18] Realism's practical emphasis on human sin may, however, obscure a theoretical realism that is equally important. A practical recognition of the way human beings distort reality to suit their own purposes must never shade over into a denial that there is a reality which they distort. The theological idealism that reduces all accounts of the world and its order to an "objectification of my own Babylonian heart"[19] forfeits its claim to speak realistically about that world in a practical sense as well. A practical Christian realism must also be realist in the sense that Thomistic moral theology is realist. It insists that a comprehensive account of human life is possible and that only the knowledge of the human reality—what it tends toward as well as what it presently is—can guide specific choices for action.

As American Protestants have sought more adequate systematic and theological foundations for the political concerns of Christian realism, they have discovered their continuity with the traditions of natural law.[20] European Protestants who seek to avoid a simple identification of Christian ethics and radical politics have been led in similar directions.[21]

What marks this new realism, Protestant and Catholic,[22] is a readiness to engage with others on the particulars of choice and action while frankly acknowledging the comprehensive impact of its own theocentric understanding of reality. When it comes to measuring the effects of a social policy or to understanding the pressures that shape a decision about medical treatment, a contemporary Christian realism claims no special insight. When we ask, however, which set of outcomes is genuinely good for persons or what decision-making procedures best respect the humanity of both patient and physician, the Christian realist insists that he or she cannot answer that question without recourse to the traditions of faith that describe Christ's formation and re-formation in human history. What saves this recourse from mere confessionalism is a corollary insistence that no one else can escape a similar move, either. In place of a dichotomy between "secular ethics" that seeks a consensus without ultimate agreement and "religious ethics" that derives all imperatives from supraempirical truths, realism today seeks a unified moral discourse which holds everyone accountable to what can be known about the facts and excuses no one from communicating plainly the ultimate context in which he or she believes the facts are set. If the original formulations of Christian realism worried most about a liberal, democratic idealism that ignored the realities of evil, contemporary Christian realism faces above all a pragmatic secularism that refuses to articulate its own faith and reduces all questions of value to questions of individual or group interest which can be negotiated.

Choices and Conclusions

Neither Bonhoeffer nor Brunner provides us with a full account of theological realism adequate to our own day. That would require a more complete examination of the realism in Roman Catholic moral theology and the American Protestant realists who first popularized the term 'Christian realism'. What the present study of European Protestantism does is cheifly to clarify the choices that confront Christian social ethics when we have no more easy understandings of faith and culture on which to presume. Barth, Brunner, and Bonhoeffer not only undermine the syntheses of earlier theology. They establish the parameters of choice for the uneasy situation that follows—the freedom of a "confessing church" or the "critical cooperation" of a church that takes its place within the orders of creation, the radicalism of obedience to the "prominent lines" of Jesus' teaching or the realism that seeks responsible ways to make God's will effective in present historical circumstances. The authors and events we have studied put the decision before us and expose the opportunities and dangers that each choice offers.

Those who choose an ethic of obedience that mistrusts all prevailing systems and stresses the radical implications of discipleship are most secure in the freedom without which the church cannot exist. Because they insist on the distinction between faith and culture, they are in little danger of identifying some local, temporary aspiration with the truth of Christianity; but because they regard all human systems with equal suspicion, they may overlook possibilities for social change and avenues of influence on society that really are open to them.

Realists, by contrast, are in danger of accepting what happens momentarily to be real as inevitable and necessary and of treating what they regard as necessary as also necessarily good. To avoid that snare, Christians must nurture a vision of reality in which Christ takes form in history, and they must retain the freedom to act on that vision even when the powers that prevail in state, or labor, or culture see reality in quite another way. The need for these "ventures of responsibility" occasionally or even often does not, however, create for the realist a state of permanent opposition between faith and social order. The ventures that sometimes set church against society and faith against culture must not become boundary markers for a permanent separation. The realist expects instead that when Christians truly understand their solutions for society's problems they will be able also to articulate them in ways that can win general assent; and when that Christian social vision must be transformed into historical realities and specific decisions, realists understand their dependence on the skill and cooperation of others whose visions and affirmations may for the moment be quite different.

Barth, Brunner, and Bonhoeffer, by what they did and what they taught, set the choice of radicalism or realism before us; and they remind us that either choice can be made in faith. If the German Christians alone had spoken of the importance of the created order for the Christian life, Protestantism after 1945 would no doubt have rejected all appeals to the natural with a vehemence that would have made Barth's "No!" seem reticent by comparison. If only political radicals had asserted the inadequacy of all social systems and the necessity of a moral commitment that is not weakened by loyalty to any existing interests, postwar Christian ethics might have adhered to the culture of liberal capitalism with a tenacity that would have made the old Prussian union of throne and altar look loose indeed. If there were no Barth but only Brunner and Bonhoeffer; or if there were no Brunner nor Bonhoeffer but only Barth, the range of choices before us in Christian ethics today would be more narrow but also less adequate to the variety of situations in which the church today must exist.

It is by setting those options squarely before us that these men mark our path. Certainly, they do not define a unified, neoorthodox school of theological ethics. As we have seen, each of them has connections with the thought of theologians and moral philosophers outside the Protestant tradition, and often the distance that separates Barth or Brunner or Bonhoeffer from a Catholic moral theologian or an existentialist philosopher is less than the distance that separates one of the Protestants from another.

What unites Barth, Brunner, and Bonhoeffer is the urgency of the question of faith and society that confronted them and the clarity of the answers they put before us. They show us the choices we must make about the meaning of our life in church and society before our decisions about more specific issues of justice and social policy can make any sense, and by their persistent attention to fundamental questions of moral theology, they demonstrate the power of a Christian theological response to situations of social crisis. Political coalitions, legal stratagems, diplomacy, public declarations, and even conspiracy were all employed in the attempt to meet the crises that defeat and dictatorship forced upon the churches, but these were never seen as emergency interruptions of the church's task, designed only to cope with the situation until the distinctively theological work could be resumed. The struggle for democracy and a humane economic order, the controversy with the German Christians, and even the conspiracy against Hitler were all understood immediately in theological terms. The continuing power of Barth, Brunner, and Bonhoeffer testifies to the importance of meeting social problems with an analysis that includes theology and indeed encompasses economics, sociology, and politics in a theological understanding of reality. In the ninth decade of our century as in the third, fourth, and fifth, the church serves best in social crisis, not by suspending its theological labors, but by intensifying them.

NOTES

1. Stanley Hauerwas, *A Community of Character* (Notre Dame, Ind.: University of Notre Dame Press, 1981), 1.

2. John Francis Kavanaugh, *Following Christ in a Consumer Society* (Maryknoll, N.Y.: Orbis Books, 1981). See also Dorothee Soelle, "'Thou Shalt Have No Other Jeans Before Me': The Need for Liberation in a Consumerist Society," in *The Challenge of Liberation Theology: A First World Response,* ed. Brian Mahan and L. Dale Richesin (Maryknoll, N.Y.: Orbis Books, 1981), 4–16.

3. Barth, *How to Serve God,* 66–67.

4. Enda McDonagh, *Doing the Truth: The Quest for Moral Theology* (Notre Dame, Ind.: University of Notre Dame Press, 1979), 34.

5. John Howard Yoder, *The Politics of Jesus* (Grand Rapids: Wm. B. Eerdmans, 1972), 141.

6. Stanley Hauerwas, "From System to Story," In *Truthfulness and Tragedy* (Notre Dame, Ind.: University of Notre Dame Press, 1979), 34.

7. See, for example, Alasdair MacIntyre, *After Virtue* (Notre Dame, Ind.: University of Notre Dame Press, 1981).

8. Barth, *The Holy Ghost,* 110–13.

9. Yoder, *Politics of Jesus,* 72.

10. European interpreters of Barth, particularly, have sought a foundation in his work for a radical politics that would continue the emphasis on social change that dominated Barth's early, pre–World War I interest in religious socialism. See George Hunsinger, ed., *Karl Barth and Radical Politics* (Philadel-

phia: Westminster Press, 1976); also Friedrich-Wilhelm Marquardt, *Theologie und Sozialismus: Das Beispiel Karl Barths* (Munich and Mainz: Kaiser/Grünewald, 1972).

11. Yoder, *Politics of Jesus,* 153.

12. Bonhoeffer, *Ethics,* 143–49; Brunner, *Justice,* 85–95.

13. An influential jurist's statement, interesting in this context because the author was Bonhoeffer's brother-in-law, may be found in Gerhard Leibholz, *Politics and Law* (London: A. W. Sythoff, 1965), 20–23.

14. A sharper criticism was the charge that an unscrupulous casuist could always find *some* general principle that would justify the desired course of action, but this argument amounts to the claim that those who used the system of moral theology did so in bad faith rather than to a criticism of the moral theology itself.

15. George Hunsinger has suggested that the more general guidelines for action indicated in Barth's later works might also be interpreted as "middle axioms." See George Hunsinger, "Karl Barth and Radical Politics: Some Further Considerations," *Studies in Religion/Sciences Religieuses,* 7 (1978): 167–91.

16. W. A. Visser 't Hooft and J. H. Oldham, *The Church and Its Function in Society* (Chicago: Willett-Clark, 1937), 210. A more extended treatment of middle axioms is provided by John C. Bennett, *Christian Ethics and Social Policy* (New York: Charles Scribner's Sons, 1946), 77–83.

17. See chapter 3, 68.

18. Reinhold Niebuhr, *Christian Realism,* 119.

19. Helmut Thielicke, *Theological Ethics* (Philadelphia: Fortress Press, 1966), 1, xxi.

20. See especially Paul Ramsey, *Nine Modern Moralists* (New York: Charles Scribner's Sons, 1962); and James Gustafson, *Protestant and Roman Catholic Ethics: Prospects for Rapprochement* (Chicago: University of Chicago Press, 1978).

21. See, for example, Wolfhart Pannenberg, "On the Theology of Law," in *Ethics* (Philadelphia: Westminster Press, 1981), 23–56. Pannenberg's persistent reservations about traditional formulations of natural law are reflected in his comment that contemporary interpretations display "the actual meaning, the truth of natural law, of which the originators of the doctrines of natural law remained largely unaware" (p. 50). His primary reason for a new appreciation of natural law is that its Protestant critics have provided no alternative to positivism.

22. Just as Protestants have been giving new attention to natural law, Catholic authors have recently noted the relevance of Protestant Christian realism for further development of their social ethics. See David Hollenbach, "Public Theology in America: Some Questions for Catholicism after John Courtney Murray," *Theological Studies* 37 (1976): 290–303; and Dennis McCann, *Christian Realism and Liberation Theology: Practical Theologies in Conflict* (Maryknoll, N.Y.: Orbis Books, 1981).

INDEX

179

CEDS LIBRARY

32114081